The most important decis
his or her response
This book asks the ques
I believe
I hope in readi
will reach ...

– **Jonathan Edwards**
Triple Jump World Record holder,
Olympic Champion, Sydney 2000

Thoroughly researched. Beautifully and yet simply
written... I was touched by the book.
– **Sue, Hitchin, Herts**

The book occupies pride of place on my humble bookshelf
in my cell having been read and re-read not just by myself
but a few other inmates to whom I have passed it on.
It is well researched and filled with fascinating anecdotes,
divine inspiration and as such is a wonderful
prescription for a complete life.
– **From a prisoner who has read**
Cure for Life and recently found Jesus

Cure
for Life

BERNARD PALMER

Published by
CHRISTIAN MEDICAL FELLOWSHIP
London England

CURE FOR LIFE

Copyright © 1996 by Bernard Palmer.

First published 1996 by Summit Publishing Ltd., Milton Keynes, England.

This edition published 2002 by Christian Medical Fellowship, 157 Waterloo Road, London SE1 8XN, England.

British Library Cataloguing-in-Publication data. Catalogue record for this book is available from the British Library.

Quotations in each chapter are from the following:

Ch. 1: *Mere Christianity* by C. S. Lewis, Fontana, 1956, pages 40–41.
Ch. 3: *Evidence that Demands a Verdict* by Josh McDowell, Campus Crusade, 1972, pages 190–191.
Ch. 4: *Is the New Testament History?* by Paul Barnett, Hodder and Stoughton, 1986, page 17.
Evidence for Jesus by R. T. France, Hodder and Stoughton, 1986, page 21.
New Bible Dictionary, InterVarsity Press, 1962.
The History of Christianity, ed. Tim Dowley, Lion Publishing, 1977.
Ch. 7: *My God is Real* by David Watson, Kingsway Publications, 1970, page 80.
Ch. 9: *Practical Religion* by J. C. Ryle, James Clarke, 1959, page 87.
Ch. 10: *Questions of Life* by Nicky Gumbell, Kingsway, 1995, page 193.

Cover design by Paul Jones.
Cover photograph - Wellcome Photo Library.

Although every effort has been made to locate the source of quoted material, some may have been inadvertently omitted, these will be rectified in future editions of this work.

ISBN: 0-906747-33-3

All Scripture quotations, unless otherwise indicated, are taken from the HOLY BIBLE, NEW INTERNATIONAL VERSION® NIV®. Copyright © 1973, 1978, 1984 by International Bible Society. Used by permission.

Reproduced, printed and bound in Great Britain for Christian Medical Fellowship by Stanley L Hunt (Printers) Ltd, Midland Road, Rushden, Northants.

Acknowledgements

The Christian life has been described as a relay race through the generations. I would really like to thank all those who have helped pass on the baton to me. My parents introduced me to the Christian boys' camps run by Lymington Holidays. The leaders there sowed the seeds that germinated when I was an undergraduate at Downing College, Cambridge. I would also like to thank the Christians in the University, the many visiting Christian teachers who came to the Christian Union and the Round Church, and particularly the late David Watson who was a curate at the Round and encouraged me greatly in my growth as a young Christian.

Since then it has been those such as Francis Schaeffer, Dick Lucas and Don Carson, who have faithfully taught me the Bible and helped me to think more like Jesus, who have had most influence. It is primarily from the Bible that we know how much God loves us and how his Spirit can change people, and experience amply supports that this is what he is doing today. Thank you to all those whose books and talks have been scoured for the material of this book, which simply summarises what they have taught me.

The 'Christian Basics' course from which this book is derived was developed with John Parsons, Vicar of St. Paul's, Letchworth. The idea and original scripts came from Daphne Rance who was on one of the courses. The text has been refined by many, including my parents and good friends Jonathan Welch and Derek Moore-Crispin. Dorothy Fletcher and Hazel Barrett helped with the typing.

Finally my family have been a tower of strength. My fabulous wife, Rosy, has been a constant source of encouragement and helpful comments. Robert suggested the title, and Sam, Rachel and Andrew have made helpful contributions. A young family is also a great incentive to practise what you teach!

Contents

*"Is there a God?
I think there is but I'm not really sure."*

Chapter 1

WHY BOTHER
WITH JESUS?

Brian was a patient of mine who had just been diagnosed as having secondary cancer in his liver, causing him to become jaundiced. He and his wife realised that the outlook was not good. After talking about possible treatment options, I asked Brian, "Do you have a faith that helps you at a time like this?"

He turned to his wife and asked, "Do we, dear?"

As there didn't appear to be much concern about spiritual things I simply said, "For me, knowing that there is a God who loves us and cares for us is the only thing that makes sense of problems like this," and changed the subject.

The following week, however, I met Brian as he sat in the waiting room for a blood test. He said, "You know what you said last week – it is strange but my next-door neighbour, who is a Christian, asked us if we would like to go to church. What do you think?"

"I think that is lovely, but honestly, Brian, I wonder if sitting through some hymns, prayers and a sermon is what you most need at the moment. I would guess what you most need to know is 'How can I get right with God?' "

There was a two-second pause before Brian looked up and asked, "How do I get right with God?"

We arranged to meet up the following morning at his home and there we went over the basics of the Christian faith. After a few days, first Brian and then his wife became a Christian.

Such experiences have made me certain that there is a growing number of people who, although disillusioned with churches, have many questions they would like resolved. Even the sceptic Bernard Levin has written in *The Times,* "There are probably more people today seeking some larger meaning or purpose in their lives and in life in general than there have been, certainly in the West, since the day of unquestioned faith."

Where should people begin the search for answers?

Start with God

There is an Italian proverb which says, "He who leaves God out of his reasoning has forgotten how to count." Today many consider that it is arrogant to assert anything confidently. It may be your opinion that one plus one is two, but you must not say it too loudly as others holding another view may not agree. This book unashamedly looks at the answers that Jesus gave. He taught "with great authority" that God really does matter and that the gulf that exists between God and ourselves can be bridged. Jesus himself claimed to be the one and only way to God, and that he alone has made God known. Some of Jesus' teaching is very startling and it does demand action. It is therefore an important study for everyone.

What is a Christian?

Primarily, a Christian is Christ's man or Christ's woman – a person committed to a personal relationship with God, through his Son, Jesus. Today there is a terrible misunderstanding that suggests that anyone who is particularly kind, honest and generally moral is Christian. This is not what Jesus himself taught; he was very clear as to how a person could be acceptable to God. Our great need today is for people to hear Christ's teaching, to be convinced of its truth, and then go out and live it. First, however, it is important to sort out exactly who Jesus was – or is.

Who was Jesus?

The disciples who lived very closely with Jesus became convinced that Jesus was someone very special indeed, and they wrote down what caused them to come to this conclusion. For example, in the first half of Mark's gospel there are several stories, witnessed at first hand, about this remarkable man.

1. He had power over the forces of nature
The disciples were sailing with Jesus across the Sea of Galilee when:

A furious squall came up, and the waves broke over the boat, so that it was nearly swamped. Jesus was in the stern, sleeping on a cushion. The disciples woke him and said to him, "Teacher, don't you care if we drown?"

He got up, rebuked the wind and said to the waves, "Quiet! Be still!" Then the wind died down and it was completely calm.

He said to the disciples, "Why are you so afraid? Do you still have no faith?"

(Mark 4:37–40)

Then, just as we would have, they asked, "Who is this? Even the wind and the waves obey him!"

2. He had the ability to heal physical illness and even defeat death

A man of considerable status and authority hurried up to Jesus, dropped to his knees, and pleaded desperately with him. Jairus was one of the synagogue rulers and to see him behaving so humbly before Jesus was in itself astonishing to the bystanders.

"My little daughter is dying. Please come and put your hands on her so that she will be healed and live." So Jesus went with him.

(Mark 5:23–4)

Jesus was delayed by the great crowd that pressed around him, and before he could get to the child, some men came from Jairus' house with awful news.

"Your daughter is dead," they said. "Why bother the teacher any more?"

Ignoring what they said, Jesus told the synagogue ruler, "Don't be afraid; just believe."

He did not let anyone follow him except Peter, James and John the brother of James. When they came to the home of the synagogue ruler, Jesus saw a commotion, with people crying and wailing loudly. He went in and said to them, "Why all this commotion and wailing? The child is not dead but asleep." But they laughed at him.

After he put them all out, he took the child's hand and said to her, "*Talitha koum!*" (which means "Little girl, I say to you, get up!"). Immediately the girl stood up and walked around (she was twelve years old).

(Mark 5:35–42)

The people were "completely astonished" by this man, who could bring the dead back to life. The disciples were beginning to understand who this extraordinary man was.

3. He claimed power to forgive sins

Jesus was preaching in the town of Capernaum, at the northern end of the Sea of Galilee. When people heard he was there, they came crowding in to listen until the house was overflowing.

Some men came, bringing to him a paralytic, carried by four of them. Since they could not get him to Jesus because of the crowd, they made an opening in the roof above Jesus and, after digging through it, lowered the mat the paralysed man was lying on. When Jesus saw their faith, he said to the paralytic, "Son, your sins are forgiven."

Now some teachers of the law were sitting there, thinking to themselves, "Why does this fellow talk like that? He's blaspheming! Who can forgive sins but God alone?"

(Mark 2:3–7)

What was Jesus claiming? We can all forgive individuals who offend us, but obviously only God can forgive offending against God. If Jesus were not God then his claim to forgive sin would indeed be blasphemous. To demonstrate that he had God's authority, he told the paralytic man to get up and go home – and the man, now whole and undoubtedly very happy, "took his mat and walked out in full view of them all. This amazed everyone and they praised God, saying, 'We have never seen anything like this.' " (verse 12) He was claiming to be God!

Some people do not believe that they ever sin – but the truth is that we *all* do. It is easily explained through the game of archery. In this sport, when the arrow falls short of the target it is termed a "sin": the arrow has failed to hit its intended mark. In just the same way in our everyday lives we all fall short of God's target, the target being God's standards: " . . . for all have sinned and fall short of the glory of God" (Romans 3:23).

4. He said he was God

The four contemporary biographers of Jesus had no doubt who Jesus claimed to be. In Mark's record, there are two climaxes. The first is when Jesus asks his disciples who he really is, and Peter answers, "You are the Christ" (Mark 8:29). The second was at his trial before the High Priest when he was asked bluntly, "Are you the Christ, the son of the Blessed One?" The reply was clarity itself, "I am, and you will see the Son of Man sitting at the right hand of the Mighty One" (Mark 14:61–2). The word Christ means the same as Messiah or "Anointed One". It was the term used in the sacred writings of the Jews, our Old Testament, of the eternal King of God's people who would rule with perfect justice for ever. A staggering claim!

John recorded Jesus as saying:

> " . . . I am God's Son. Do not believe me
> unless I do what the Father does. But if I
> do it, even though you do not believe me,
> believe the miracles, that you may learn and
> understand that the Father is in me, and I in
> the Father."

> *(John 10:36–8)*

It is important to realise that, when Jesus claimed to be the Son of God, he meant what Jews of his time would have meant – that he was equal with God. Fathers and sons were more closely identified than they are today; a son was one with his father, to share in his honour or revenge his wrongs. So in saying, "I am the Son of God", he was saying, "I am the incarnation of God, God in the flesh – I am God." In the past, there have been teachers who said that Jesus never claimed to be divine, but even a superficial study of the apostles' writings leaves no room for doubt.

> "I am the way and the truth and the life. No one comes to the Father except through me. If you really knew me, you would know my Father as well. From now on, you do know him and have seen him."
>
> Philip said, "Lord, show us the Father and that will be enough for us."
>
> Jesus answered, "Don't you know me, Philip, even after I have been among you such a long time? Anyone who has seen me has seen the Father. How can you say 'Show us the Father'? Don't you believe that I am in the Father, and that the Father is in me? The words that I say to you are not just my own. Rather, it is the Father, living in me, who is doing his work."
>
> *(John 14:6–10)*

Even his enemies had no doubt what Jesus was claiming. This is why, on one occasion, when Jesus said, "I and the Father are one", the Jews picked up stones to stone him.

> Jesus said to them, "I have shown you many great miracles from the Father. For which of these do you stone me?"
>
> "We are not stoning you for any of these," replied the Jews, "but for blasphemy,

because you, a mere man, claim to be God."
(John 10:30–3)

Similarly in Matthew's gospel the final confirmation came at his trial by the Sanhedrin, the ruling body of the Jews. The High Priest, Caiaphas, asked Jesus directly:

"I charge you under oath by the living God:
Tell us if you are the Christ, the Son of God."
    "Yes, it is as you say," Jesus replied.
But I say to all of you: In the future you will
see the Son of Man sitting at the right hand
of the Mighty One . . . "
(Matthew 26:63–4)

The "oath by the living God" was the most serious of Jewish oaths and had to be answered honestly. The judges condemned Jesus for blasphemy. There was no doubt in anyone's mind exactly who Jesus was claiming to be.

Was Jesus mad, bad, or God?

If you stood outside your nearest supermarket armed with a ball-point and clipboard and asked people, "Who do you think Jesus was?", what sort of answers would you get? Some might say, "Who's he?" others may reply "Don't care"; "Nothing to do with me"; but I expect many would say "a good man" or "a great moral teacher".

He was indeed a very great teacher. " . . . the crowds were amazed at his teaching, because he taught as one who had authority" (Matthew 7:28–9).

His talks were full of human stories that caught the attention but, at the same time, were exceedingly profound, touching the deepest needs of the listening men and women and giving them joy, freedom from guilt, and a new meaning and purpose in their lives.   But he was **not** just a good teacher. The writer C. S. Lewis said:

> That is one thing we must not say. A man who was merely a man and said the sort of things Jesus said would not be a great moral teacher. He would either be a lunatic – on a level with the man who says he is a poached egg – or else he would be the Devil of Hell. You must make your choice. Either this was and is the Son of God, or else a madman or something worse. You can shut him up for a fool, you can fall at his feet and call him Lord and God, but you must not come with any patronising nonsense about his being a great human teacher. He has not left that open to us.   He did not intend to.

As we have seen, Jesus claimed to be infinitely more than just a great teacher. From the accounts of what he said and did, there are only three possible conclusions. Either he was:

- BAD
- or MAD
- or GOD

Bad?

Jesus claimed to be God. If that was not true then he was lying and there is no way that a liar can be called "good" let alone "God". Furthermore, he promised benefits to his followers that he could not possibly confer if he were not God; he raised hopes that if he were not God he could not possibly sustain; he has caused the death by martyrdom of countless men and women from his day to ours – quite pointlessly, if they died for a false reason. If he were not God, then he was an utterly cruel liar and quite simply BAD. However, his friend Peter, who knew him inside out and later chose to die for him, wrote, "He committed no sin, and no deceit was found in his mouth" (1 Peter 2:22).

Mad?

If someone came up to you today and said, "I am God", what would you think? Wouldn't you back away nervously, afraid that he had escaped from the nearest mental hospital and was suffering from delusions? Other people have believed themselves to be Napoleon or the Queen of Sheba – or God; so perhaps Jesus was mentally deranged rather than deliberately wicked – in other words, MAD.

His contemporary biographers depicted Jesus as the very opposite type of person. There are no violent mood swings, depressive episodes or the schizophrenic's tendency to be out of touch with reality. On the contrary, they paint a picture of somebody who is eminently sane, balanced and reliable – a tough, compassionate, practical man who drew love and respect from all who met him.

God?

If he is neither Bad nor Mad, is he then exactly who he claimed to be – God? There is just no way that you can read the Bible and come to any other reasonable conclusion. No other recognised religious leader, such as Moses, Buddha, Mohammed or Confucius has ever claimed to be God, yet Jesus convinced those closest to him that his claims were true. One of his twelve disciples, Thomas, met Jesus a week after the resurrection and responded by saying, "My Lord and my God!" (John 20:28).

Several years later, the apostle Paul wrote to one of the next generation of Christian leaders, Titus, and referred to Jesus as "our great God and Saviour" (Titus 2:13).

Anyone who can read the books and letters collected together in what we call the New Testament and not conclude that Jesus claimed to be God – and gave very strong evidence to support this claim – and that the disciples recognised him as such, is being wilfully blind!

These claims are either the most startling news ever to break on earth, or are untrue and therefore to be denounced. Not to take any interest in this person would be absurd. In the next chapters we will study in detail the evidence that supports Christian claims.

*"I think there could have been
a person called Jesus but I believe
he was just a good man."*

Chapter 2

THE LONG
EXPECTED GODSEND

Christianity is not an ethic, a good way to live; it is a
story about Jesus who was God in the flesh. It therefore
depends absolutely on there being a real Jesus who
actually lived, who really was God, who really did die to
take away the penalty of our sins and who rose from the
dead to prove his claims. No blind leap of faith is required,
but a commitment based on evidence. That evidence
comes from many different quarters.

   A missionary in Turkey had some Muslim students
round for tea. Afterwards, he read to them the following
ancient writing and then asked them these questions:

"Who is this about?"; "Who wrote it?"; and "When was it written?";

> A man of sorrows, acquainted with bitterest grief, we turned our backs on him and looked the other way when he went by. He was despised and we did not care, yet it was our grief he bore, our sorrows that weighed him down, and we thought his troubles were a punishment from God for his own sins. But he was wounded and bruised for our sins; he was chastised that we might have peace; he was lashed and we were healed. We are the ones who strayed away like sheep, we who left God's paths to follow our own, yet God laid on him the guilt and sin of every one of us. He was oppressed and he was afflicted, yet he never said a word. He was brought as a lamb to the slaughter and, as a sheep before her shearer is dumb, so he stood silent before the ones condemning him. From prison and trial, they led him away to his death, but who among the people of that day realised it was their sins that he was dying for, that he was suffering their punishment? He was buried like a criminal, in a rich man's grave, but he had done no wrong and never spoken an evil word."

They quickly realised that this passage was about the crucifixion of Jesus, and thought that it was written by one of his early disciples because of the detail given. They were amazed to learn that it was in fact written over seven hundred years before Jesus was born by the prophet Isaiah! This passage teaches that the coming servant king would be despised, flogged, and finally killed as a wrongdoer – yet he was to do this on our behalf, to bear our sins.

Old Testament prophecies

The Old Testament contains over three hundred such prophecies about the coming Messiah – the promised deliverer of God's people who would reign for ever. These were written at widely differing times in the history of the Jewish people, and sixty of them are of major significance, like the one quoted above.

In the 1920s, a publisher in the United States of America offered $1000 to anyone who could show that even half of the prophecies could refer to someone other than Jesus. No one has ever claimed the prize and the challenge still stands.

Here are some of the Messianic prophecies:

1. His birth

The prophets predicted that the rescue mission of God would involve the birth of a special baby. This suggests that there was something extraordinary about this child right from the beginning. Note who the prophet says he will be:

> For to us a child is born, to us a son is given,
> and the government will be on his shoulders.
> And he will be called Wonderful Counsellor,
> Mighty God, Everlasting Father, Prince of

Peace. Of the increase of his government and peace there will be no end. He will reign . . . for ever.

(Isaiah 9:6–7)

Where? His birth would take place in the village of Bethlehem, five miles outside Jerusalem:

But you, Bethlehem Ephrathah, though you are small among the clans of Judah, out of you will come for me one who will be ruler over Israel, whose origins are from of old, from ancient times . . . He will stand and shepherd his flock in the strength of the Lord, in the majesty of the name of the Lord his God. And they will live securely, for then his greatness will reach to the ends of the earth. And he will be their peace.

(Micah 5:2–5)

This village only had about two hundred houses when Jesus was born. No one else of major importance has been born in Bethlehem since this prophecy was written.

When? The Messiah would come whilst the temple at Jerusalem was still standing, and would be preceded by a prophet who would prepare the people:

" See, I will send my messenger, who will prepare the way before me. Then suddenly the Lord you are seeking will come to his temple; the messenger of the covenant, whom you desire, will come," says the Lord Almighty.

(Malachi 3:1)

The temple was destroyed in AD 70 by the Romans and has never been rebuilt. This passage also hints strongly that this Messiah would be the Lord God himself! John the Baptist was to become the forerunner (Matthew 3:3).

How? He would have a remarkable conception in that his mother would be a virgin. He would have no human father, but would be the true son of God:

> Therefore the Lord himself will give you a sign: the virgin will be with child and will give birth to a son, and will call him Immanuel.
>
> *(Isaiah 7:14)*

The name Immanuel literally means "God with us", which is who Jesus claimed to be.

2. His ministry

When Jesus delivered one of his first sermons in the synagogue at Nazareth, his home town, during his ministry, he quoted another prophesy of Isaiah and applied it to himself saying:

> The Spirit of the Sovereign Lord is on me, because the Lord has anointed me to preach the good news to the poor. He has sent me to bind up the broken-hearted, to proclaim freedom for the captives and release from darkness for the prisoners, to proclaim the year of the Lord's favour and the day of vengeance of our God . . .
>
> *(Isaiah 61:1–2)*

This is particularly startling as most preachers then were concerned to influence the behaviour of the powerful and influential, not to offer a rescue package to the poor, whether their poverty was material, physical or spiritual! This is what Jesus came to do. This passage also emphasises two aspects of the future Messiah's work – firstly he would preach the good news of freedom and forgiveness, but later he would execute God's wrath on those who reject him.

3. His death

Psalm 22 was written by King David about 1012 BC. It starts with the words, "My God, my God, why have you forsaken me?" which Jesus quoted as he was about to die on the Cross. He obviously thought that this Psalm referred to him and when you read on it is not surprising.

> All who see me mock me; they hurl insults, shaking their heads: 'He trusts in the Lord; let the Lord rescue him. Let him deliver him, since he delights in him.'
>
> *(Psalm 22:7–8)*

> I am poured out like water, and all my bones are out of joint.
>
> *(Psalm 22:14)*

> . . . my tongue sticks to the roof of my mouth; you lay me in the dust of death. Dogs have surrounded me; a band of evil men has encircled me; they have pierced my hands and my feet. I can count all my bones;

people stare and gloat over me. They divide
my garments among them and cast lots for
my clothing.

(Psalm 22:15–18)

This is a very specific description of death by
crucifixion, which is all the more striking as no description
of this torture has been discovered before 300 BC when
the Phoenician people invented it! It depicts a godly man
being vilified by those watching his death. He is very
dehydrated, and his joints were out of place which were
features of such deaths, which could take up to nine days.
It even foretells the way his clothes were distributed. At a
Roman crucifixion, four soldiers were allocated to each
condemned man. They would guard him until he was
dead. One of the perks of this grisly job was to have his
personal property, which they divided up between them.
They even cast lots for the best item: the seamless
undergarment (John 19:23–4).

4. His resurrection

Although it was God's will that Jesus should die on our
behalf, it was equally his plan that death would not be the
end.

He was assigned a grave with the wicked,
and with the rich in his death, though he had
done no violence, nor was any deceit in his
mouth. Yet it was the Lord's will to crush
him and cause him to suffer, and though the
Lord makes his life a guilt offering, he will
see his offspring and prolong his days . . .

> After the suffering of his soul, he will see
> the light of life and be satisfied.
>
> *(Isaiah 53:9–11)*

This passage teaches that after his death as a guilt offering, the Messiah will live again.

5. The family history of Jesus

The whole of the Old Testament is a description of the unfolding drama of God's rescue mission of his people. The prophecies about the pedigree of God's Messiah, who would complete this rescue, are very clear. At the beginning of Matthew's gospel (Chapter 1), great importance is placed on the significance of Jesus' ancestry. Luke also stresses the importance of his family background and describes it right back to Adam. Those people mentioned include the following.

Noah, who built the ark is there. It was his son, Shem, who was to be the forefather of the Semitic (Shem-itic) people, the Jews and Arabs.

Abraham had two sons. Ishmael was the son of his servant Hagar, but later his wife Sarah had Isaac. There was bitter rivalry between the two. Ishmael became the father of the Arab people, whereas Isaac was the ancestor of the Jews. This antagonism has continued to this present day.

Isaac had twin sons: Esau the hairy hunter, and Jacob the smooth-skinned scheming farmer. They were also jealous adversaries. God's Messiah was to come through Jacob, who was renamed Israel by God. Jacob had twelve sons who were the leaders of the twelve tribes of Israel. It was prophesied that the Messiah would come from the tribe of Judah.

When the Jews entered the promised land under Joshua, they first captured the city of Jericho. The two spies who had visited the city earlier had been rescued by a young prostitute named Rahab, who had a flat in the wall of the city. Because of what she had done, she was protected when the city was routed (Joshua 2). Why should this woman have a whole chapter in the Bible? It was because she was to be an ancestor of Jesus! She married one of the soldiers of the victorious army and they had a son called Boaz.

Many have been puzzled as to why the short book of Ruth is in the Bible. After all, she was a Moabite woman. However, her second marriage was to Boaz who by this time owned land at Bethlehem. Their grandson was Jesse who became the father of King David. The prophet Jeremiah said what God thought of this family:

> I will raise up to David a righteous Branch,
> a King who will reign wisely and do what is
> just and right in the land. In his days Judah
> will be saved and Israel will live in safety.
> This is the name by which he will be called:
> The Lord Our Righteousness.
>
> *(Jeremiah 23:5–6)*

That is exactly what Jesus, the son (or descendant) of David, did; he became our righteousness.

A consultant colleague of mine asked me one day why I was a Christian. "Because it is true," I replied. We then discussed the types of evidence that there are. He became intrigued by the concept that so much about Jesus had been prophesied in the Old Testament, and set about to check up on this claim. He found many prophesies that I didn't know about! After a few months, he said "I am convinced," and soon after that he committed himself to Jesus.

Realising that the Old Testament is all about Jesus can have a profound effect on a Christian's life.

Chandu Rai was born into a caring Hindu family in India. When aged 27, he became a Christian. Within three months, his concern for his people led him to write to his bishop asking to be trained as an evangelist. The Bishop replied, "Your letter has come as a snowdrop in the wilderness," and he was sent to a theological college. After three years, he had returned with no faith, his simple trust in the Bible as God's book had been torn from him. In the first nine months of his ministry, he helped no one to become a Christian. Then a lady missionary came to him and asked "Do you believe what you preach?"

Chandu became angry, thinking, "How dare this woman talk to me like that?"

"I ask you as a sister in Christ," she gently went on.

Chandu opened his heart to her and explained that at the theological college they had taught him to doubt the reliability of the Bible. She gently helped him back to realising that the Bible really was God's word to us. In particular, he was helped by reading a book called *Christ in all the Scriptures* by A. M. Hodgkin which, in great detail, shows how the Old Testament is about Jesus from beginning to end. From that time, a week never passed when he did not help someone to become a Christian. He eventually became the Right Reverend Doctor Chandu Rai, Bishop of Karachi, but he never again lost his simple trust in his heavenly Father.

*"We all have to die – and
when you're dead,
you're dead, that's it!"*

Chapter 3

DID JESUS RISE
FROM THE DEAD?

The resurrection is the cornerstone of the Christian faith – if it did not occur, then Christianity is in tatters. The apostle Paul recognised this when he wrote: "And if Christ has not been raised, your faith is futile; you are still in your sins" (1 Corinthians 15:17).

It is the final proof that Jesus is all he claimed to be. The resurrection was prophesied in the Old Testament, foretold by Jesus in the New, and is the foundation of early church teaching. When Paul started to discuss the Christian claims on his visit to Athens, he kept talking about "Jesus and Anastasis". He was not talking about two gods, as some casual listeners supposed, but was telling them about "Jesus and the Resurrection", *anastasis* being Greek for "resurrection".

The resurrection is so central to the Christian faith that it is not surprising that several attempts have been made to explain the event away.

Was the wrong person executed?

This theory proposes that, if the wrong man was executed, it would be a simple matter for Jesus to appear fit and well and claim to have risen from the dead and so convince his gullible disciples. It is significant that this possibility was never proposed by the early opponents of the Christian faith. It is simply not tenable.

Jesus was very well known. He had been publicly tried and executed. When on the Cross, he had been seen by his mother and family, his disciples, Jewish opponents, and Roman authorities. No one had any doubt that the condemned man was Jesus, the preacher and miracle worker. When he was seen again alive on the third day, the disciples saw that he had wounds where nails had penetrated his wrists and feet, and another in his side where the spear had penetrated!

Could he have swooned on the Cross?

The *Today* newspaper of 27 April 1991 ran a startling feature on its front page, with the headline, "**JESUS DID NOT DIE ON CROSS.**" It was proposed that Jesus was still alive when taken from the Cross, and that placing him in a cool place would have revived him. This theory was first propounded at the end of the eighteenth century and has appeared every generation since. Let us look at some of the relevant facts.

1. Jesus was first subjected to a Roman flogging. He was stripped of his clothes, and his wrists were tied to the top of the pole. The instrument used was a *flagrum*, which consisted of a handle with several leather thongs, each having jagged pieces of lead tied to the ends. The shoulders, back, buttocks and legs of Jesus were repeatedly flayed by this instrument until the centurion in charge decided that Jesus had had enough. It was not uncommon for muscle to be ripped and bone to be exposed. Not surprisingly, people had died from a Roman flogging alone!

2. The condemned man had to carry the heavy crossbar of his crucifix through the city to the place of execution. It is not surprising that, after the flogging, Jesus was so weakened that he collapsed and an onlooker was commandeered to carry it for him. These crossbars were often the long pieces of strong wood used to bar doors and could weigh nearly a hundredweight. The place of crucifixion was not a "green hill far away" but was almost certainly by the side of a main road leaving the northern side of Jerusalem. This would give the maximum deterrent effect.

3. At the execution site, the upright of the crucifix was laid on the ground and the crossbar tied to it firmly. A small wooden seat was nailed to the upright. Jesus was then held down on the cross and long nails were struck through each forearm, and then one nail was hit through the calcanea, the heel bones, holding the legs in a slightly flexed position. The whole structure was then lifted up and dropped into a hole in the ground. His feet would

only be about eighteen inches off the ground.

The victims suffered severe pain and cramps in their arms and legs, and breathing became very difficult. The victim cannot keep still. If he slumps he cannot breathe in – and if he pushes up to breathe, he gets an excruciating pain from his feet. This exhausts, shocks and weakens him. The small seat helped with this regard but also prolonged the agony. The longest recorded time that anyone survived on a cross was nine days. Jesus was crucified at 9 a.m. and was dead by 3 p.m.

4. Each condemned man was guarded by four Roman soldiers. It was a capital offence for them to leave until death had occurred. If they wanted to bring on an early death, one of the soldiers would hit the lower legs with a mallet, and break the bones. This practice was called *crurifragium*. The pain, blood loss and inability to push themselves up to help breathing, rapidly brought on death. In the late afternoon on the day of Jesus' crucifixion, they did break the legs of the two thieves crucified either side of Jesus. They saw that Jesus was already dead, but, as a final check, they thrust a spear into his side. It is not possible that the soldiers could have left Jesus still alive.

5. That evening, two of the Jewish political leaders, Joseph of Arimathea and Nicodemus, who were secret disciples of Jesus, went to Pilate and asked if they could have his corpse. Pilate was surprised that Jesus had died so soon and he summoned the centurion in charge. Having the death confirmed, he gave permission for the body to be released for burial. It is inconceivable that the centurion got this wrong. He had too much to lose – it was a capital offence to make a mistake.

6. When the body was removed from the Cross, it

was taken to the recently hewn burial chamber belonging to Joseph, and it was washed according to Jewish customs, and dressed in grave clothes. They obviously had no doubt that Jesus was dead as they then embalmed the body. The embalming substance consisted of pungent aromatic spices called "aloes", made by pounding fragrant wood into dust, mixed with a sticky resin called "myrrh". Seventy-five pounds of spices alone were used. This would have been enough to give a permanent general anaesthetic to the fittest man, let alone a corpse! The body was then wrapped in white linen up to the neck, with a separate head cloth to support the jaw. It was extremely difficult to remove this resin from the skin, yet, after his resurrection, no mention is made of the odour or stickiness that would normally still be present even after multiple baths!

7. The opening of the tomb was closed with "a very large stone". One ancient manuscript of Mark's gospel adds, "which twenty men could not roll away". On the third morning, three ladies came to the tomb to add some more spices to Jesus' body, but recognised that three of them would have no chance of rolling back that stone. There is no way, therefore, that Jesus could have naturally done this.

8. The tomb was formally sealed by stretching a cord across the stone, fixing both ends with clay which were stamped with the Roman Governor's insignia. A Roman guard then protected the tomb. This guard was probably the standard guard of sixteen soldiers. Four of these would have been on duty at any time, but the others needed to be available for back-up. Matthew records that, after the resurrection, some of these guards reported what had happened to the chief priests. Presumably, they were

looking for Jewish support, so that they would put in a good word with the Roman authorities, as the soldiers had failed in their responsibilities and faced serious penalties. After a high-level meeting of the Jewish leaders, they were given a large sum of money and were told to say that the disciples had come in the night and had stolen the body whilst they were asleep. No wonder it had to be a large bribe! It is very difficult to conceive how the disciples could have outwitted an armed Roman guard in this way.

9. The breaking of a Roman seal was automatically investigated and those responsible would be punished by crucifixion upside down. It is significant that no action was taken in this case!

10. On the Sunday morning, Mary Magdalene went early to the tomb and found the stone had been moved well away from the entrance of the tomb. She ran to tell Peter and John, who also came running. There in the tomb were the strips of grave clothes still lying in their place, with the head cloth next to them. As soon as John saw this, he believed that the resurrection had taken place. The position of the clothes gave no other alternative.

11. When Jesus appeared to Mary Magdalene and, later that evening, to the other disciples, they had no doubt that Jesus had been resurrected. He was not in the dazed, ill state that he would be in if he had recovered from three days' unconsciousness. They studied his wounds – it was the same man.

12. On that first Sunday afternoon, Jesus joined two disciples as they walked to their home in Emmaus. Emmaus was seven miles away from Jerusalem. Jesus talked with these two all the way there, discussing all the Old Testament prophecies about the Messiah. It was only

when they entered their home and sat down for some food that they recognised who it was. He obviously had no odour from the embalming resin on him. As a doctor, I find this story very striking. Have you ever tried to walk with a twisted ankle? I cannot see how Jesus could normally have walked even two yards after having a large Roman nail driven through both his ankles, let alone the fourteen miles to Emmaus and back, and not hobble!

13. The final proof that Jesus must have died on the cross is one I find utterly convincing. It comes from one sentence in John's record of the crucifixion:

> Instead one of the soldiers pierced Jesus' side
> with a spear, bringing a sudden flow of blood
> and water. The man who saw it has given
> testimony, and his testimony is true.
> *(John 19:34)*

Out of the spear wound came a flow of first blood and then water. This must have collected in one of the body cavities of Jesus. We do know that the blood of animals and humans that are tortured to death does not clot (this is due to circulating anti-clotting chemicals called "fibrinolysins"). When blood is left to stand, it separates into the red cells which drop to the bottom, leaving the clear plasma above. There seems to be no other reasonable explanation of what John saw, other than that the spear pierced a large cavity which had filled up with blood just before Jesus died and that this blood had separated into the red cells and plasma. It would take at least half an hour after death for this separation to occur. It could not have occurred if Jesus had swooned.

I am interested in which cavity the spear could have

hit. The inside of the heart itself is too small to contain enough blood to produce this effect. The only other possibilities are the cavities around the lung (pleural cavity), and the cavity around the heart (pericardial cavity). Just before Jesus died, he "cried out with a loud voice". When people have a pleural cavity full of fluid, they are gasping for breath – so this does not fit. The only viable possibility is that, just before he died, there was a tear in his heart which led to a rapid filling of the pericardial space with blood. This itself would rapidly stop the heart due to what doctors call "cardiac tamponade". It is interesting that Jesus did die a "cardiac type" death – he was not comatosed but awake when he realised something was going wrong, and said "It is finished", and suddenly died. It therefore seems likely that Jesus literally died of a broken heart!

Three days after his execution Jesus appeared to the disciples and convinced them of his resurrection. That same afternoon he walked with two disciples to the village of Emmaus, which is seven miles from Jerusalem. Late that evening he joined his disciples back in Jerusalem. That means he would have had to walk 14 miles. The pain would make this totally impossible, without a miracle, because a thick Roman nail had just been driven through his feet!

From all the information that we have, from several sources, there can be no doubt that Jesus did die on that Cross.

The disciples and others were convinced

After his resurrection, Jesus appeared to many different people in different ways. He first appeared to a solitary woman, Mary Magdalene, whose testimony was not legally valid. Details such as this give the story great authenticity. If the story was invented, a first appearance to a man would have made the story more emphatic and impressive. He then appeared to the two depressed disciples walking home to Emmaus, and they were convinced. His final appearance on that first Sunday was to the disciples meeting secretly behind locked doors; they were thrilled to see Jesus again. Only Thomas was missing, and, subsequently, he was sceptical about the other disciples' accounts and insisted that he could not accept the resurrection unless he saw Jesus and his wounds for himself. Thomas was present when Jesus joined them again the following Sunday, when Jesus said to him: "Stop doubting and believe." Thomas said to him, "My Lord and my God." Then Jesus told him, "Because you have seen me, you have believed; blessed are those who have not seen and yet have believed" (John 20:27–9).

After this, he appeared to over five hundred Christians at the same time. Paul describes this in 1 Corinthians (15:6), adding that many of those were still alive at the time he wrote that letter (about AD 54). These people could still be called on to act as witnesses!

One of the most telling pieces of evidence is what happened to these followers of Jesus after they had seen him. Prior to the death of Jesus, they had been weak and uncertain. They became utterly convinced, spending the rest of their lives convincing the world about the facts as they saw them. Eleven out of the twelve apostles were probably martyred because of their convictions. Only John died naturally, and he had suffered as a prisoner on the island of Patmos. This behaviour is not explicable unless they were sure. People may live a lie but they will not die for a lie.

It was not only to his followers that Jesus appeared. Saul was an arch-enemy of the early Christians, and was directing their persecution on behalf of the Jewish leaders. He met Jesus as he was travelling to Damascus. This meeting so convinced him that he spent the rest of his life, often at great personal risk, passing on the Christian message. He was also executed by beheading just outside Rome.

James was the younger half-brother of Jesus, who had mocked Jesus during his three-year teaching ministry. Who would be more difficult to convince than a younger brother? After the resurrection, Jesus appeared specifically to him. He was convinced, and eventually became the leader of the church in Jerusalem. James wrote the epistle bearing that name in the New Testament, but was eventually stoned to death because of his convictions. Such men must have been certain to have persisted, with such determination and courage, against such odds.

At the first major sermon given by Peter, seven weeks after the death and resurrection of Jesus, Peter stressed these two facts saying: "But God raised him from the dead" (Acts 2:24).

Those listening must have known all about these events because, when they were challenged to make a decision as to who Jesus really was, about three thousand people accepted the message and were publicly baptised as followers of Jesus the Messiah. Jewish people would not do such a thing lightly.

How else can the rapid growth of the early Christian church be explained? Those people must have been certain to have risked everything they had, including their lives, to tell others of God's intervention in the world.

The nineteenth-century lawyer, Lord Lyttleton, who

was once Attorney General and three times Lord Chancellor, said: "I know pretty well what evidence is, and I tell you that such evidence as that for the resurrection has never broken down yet."

Thomas Arnold was a Professor of History at Oxford, who specialised in Roman times. He was also the famous headmaster of Rugby school. He said:

> I have been used for many years to studying the histories of other times, and to examining and weighing the evidence of those who have written about them, and I know of no one fact in the history of mankind which is proved by better and fuller evidence of every sort, to the understanding of a fair enquirer, than the great sign which God has given us that Christ died and rose again from the dead.

Chapter 4

THE JESUS
OF HISTORY

Although Jesus was executed in his early thirties in a backwater of the Roman Empire, he made so great an impact that much was written about him both by his followers and by others not so sympathetic! We will first look at some of the direct evidence for the historical Jesus by non-Christian writers.

Cornelius Tacitus

Tacitus wrote his *Annals* about AD 115. He describes how the early Christians had become such an embarrassment in Rome that the emperor Nero made them the scapegoats for the great fire of Rome that devastated the city in AD 64 – just over thirty years after the death of Jesus. There was a rumour going about that Nero himself had started the fire.

> To dispel the rumour, Nero substituted as culprits, and treated with the most extreme punishments, some people, popularly known as Christians, whose disgraceful activities were notorious. The originator of that name, Christus, had been executed when Tiberius was Emperor by order of the procurator, Pontius Pilatus. But the deadly cult, though checked for a time, was now breaking out again not only in Judea, the birthplace of this evil, but even throughout Rome, where all the nasty and disgusting ideas from all over the world pour in and find a ready following.
>
> *(Tacitus,* Annals *XV.44)*

Tacitus was obviously no friend of the Christians, but his evidence is therefore even more reliable. He confirms that Jesus lived in Judea, and was executed by order of Pontius Pilate who was governor during the period AD 26–36.

Pliny the Younger

Pliny was sent to govern Bithynia, a small state in

northern Turkey, in about AD 112. He wrote letters on
many subjects to the emperor Trajan. One of these
concerned the problem he faced with the Christians in
the area. He complained that, because of the new religion,
people were deserting the pagan temples; that the sacred
festivals were being discontinued for lack of popular
support, and that the lucrative trade in animals for temple
sacrifices was dwindling badly! He therefore had the
custom of arresting any Christians he could find and, if
they persisted in their allegiance to Jesus after being
warned of the consequences, he had them executed. Pliny
discovered that true Christians would rather die than pray
to the pagan gods, or "curse Christ", or make an offering
to the emperor's statue. He described the habits of these
early Christians.

> They were in the habit of meeting before
> dawn on a fixed day, when they would recite,
> in turn, a hymn to Christ as to a god, and
> would bind themselves by oath, not for any
> criminal act but rather that they would not
> commit any theft, robbery or adultery, nor
> betray any trust nor refuse to restore a deposit
> on demand. This done, they would disperse,
> and then they would meet again later to eat
> together (but the food was quite ordinary and
> harmless).

Pliny added that this "perverse religious cult" was
affecting "large numbers of all classes". Obviously,
something very strong indeed was convincing these
people to risk death by continuing their allegiance to Jesus.

Josephus

Josephus was a commander of the Jewish forces in the north of Judea when the Jews revolted against Rome in AD 66. He wrote two important histories. The *Antiquities* gave a history of the Jews up to AD 66, and the *The Jewish War* gives a detailed account of the rebellion between AD 66 AD 73. He was able to do this as, realising the eventual outcome, he had changed sides and became advisor on Jewish affairs to the Roman generals! He talks about many historical figures, including Pontius Pilate, John the Baptist, Herod, Caiaphas the High Priest, and James the brother of Jesus who became an early martyr when leading the church in Jerusalem. He wrote:

> At that time, there was a wise man called Jesus, and his conduct was good and he was known to be virtuous. Many among the Jews and the other nations became his disciples. Pilate condemned him to be crucified and to die, but those who had become his disciples did not abandon his discipleship. They reported that he appeared to them three days after his crucifixion and that he was alive. Accordingly he was perhaps the Messiah concerning whom the prophets have reported wonders; and the tribe of Christians, so named after him, have not disappeared to this day.
>
> *(Antiquities XVIII 63)*

Elsewhere, Josephus acknowledged that Jesus was "a

he began his archaeological studies in Turkey, he had no
confidence in the historicity of the New Testament records.
However, he gradually began to realise that Luke, who
wrote both the gospel and the Acts of the Apostles, was
always right when new information became available. He
finally concluded:

> Luke is a historian of the first rank; not
> merely are his statements of fact trustworthy,
> he is possessed of the true historical sense
> . . . in short, this author should be placed
> along the very greatest of historians.

Let us look at one example. In Acts 13:7, Luke
describes Sergius Paulus as "proconsul" of Cyprus. Sir
William Ramsay described, in 1912, a recently found
stone which had the following inscription engraved on it
in Latin:

> To L[ucius] Sergius **Paullus** the younger,
> Son of Lucius, one of four commissioners
> in charge of the Roman streets, tribune of
> the soldiers of the sixth legion.

This does support the presence of such a man, but he
is not a proconsul and his name is spelt with a double "l".
Later, however, Luke's reliability was confirmed when
an old coin was found in Cyprus bearing the inscription:
"In the proconsulship of Paulus." Note that only one 'l'
was used here!

So much has been written on the reliability of the
biblical records. Again and again, the Bible has been
proved to be the most reliable source book about ancient

times. An eminent Jewish archaeologist, Nelson Glueck, has said, "It may be stated categorically that no archaeological discovery has ever controverted a biblical reference."

There is also no ancient book for which there is anything like the same evidence to confirm that what we now hold is the same as was originally given. Over 20,000 ancient manuscripts containing all or part of the New Testament documents have been discovered so far. In contrast, we have only two manuscripts of the writings of Tacitus and seven of the writings of Pliny the Younger! Even Homer's *Iliad* has only 643 manuscripts.

In spite of all these manuscripts, the differences in the texts are few. Over 99.5 per cent of the text of the New Testament has no alternative wording. Sir Frederic Kenyon, who was director of the British Museum, wrote in his book *Our Bible and the Ancient Manuscripts*: "No fundamental doctrine of the Christian faith rests on a disputed reading."

The dating of these manuscripts is also important. Pliny first published his *History* in AD 77 but the earliest manuscript is about AD 850. Tacitus wrote his *Annals* in about AD 100, yet the earliest manuscript is AD 950. Of the ten manuscripts we have for Caesar's *Gallic Wars*, the earliest is around AD 850. The earliest New Testament document is probably the *John Rylands Fragment*, which is a small piece of papyrus containing five verses from John's gospel, chapter eighteen. It was probably copied around AD 125. The *Chester Beatty Papyri*, contain most of the New Testament, and the *Bodmer Papyri*, containing a copy of John's gospel and most of Luke's gospel were both written about AD 200. The *Codex Vaticanus* contains papyri with most of the Bible, written about AD 350. The

Codex Sinaiticus was also written in the mid fourth century and contains virtually all the New Testament and the majority of the Old. In all there are over 5,000 Greek manuscripts, and over 10,000 Latin manuscripts of parts of the New Testament, besides over 36,000 quotes from the New Testament in the writings of the early church fathers. It is on such extensive evidence that we can be confident that the New Testament we have is the same as was originally written.

Sir Frederick Kenyon also said:

> It cannot be too strongly asserted that in substance the text of the Bible is certain! . . . The number of manuscripts of the New Testament, of early translations of it, of quotations from it, is so large that it is practically certain that the true reading of every doubtful passage is preserved in some one or other of the ancient authorities. This can be said of no other ancient book in the world.

The Early Spread of Christianity

In 1945, an undisturbed tomb was found near Jerusalem. Inside were the bones of five people. The tomb had been sealed in AD 50, a coin of that date having been left inside. On one of the caskets were written the words, "Jesus, help," and on another was the inscription, "Jesus, let him arise." This find not only confirms the early spread of the Christian faith, Jesus having been crucified around AD 30, but also confirms that they recognised who Jesus was – the man who is God who holds the keys to eternal destiny.

The Christian faith spread rapidly in those early years, not by armed force as Islam did, but against great opposition. These early Christians were liable to lose their jobs and even their lives if they were followers of Jesus, yet those becoming Christians increased rapidly. What was it that convinced so many?

The major argument used by the apostles and others as to why all should become Christians was that the message about Jesus was true. Jesus had clearly stated who he was and what he had come to do. His remarkable character supported his claim, but it was the miracles, and especially the resurrection, that so many people had seen, that really proved it.

It is not a blind faith that they and we are asked to hold, but a faith based on irrefutable fact. Any honest person who rejects Jesus will have to find an explanation for all the various lines of evidence in support of his claim.

Changed Lives Today

One of the main reasons that I was inclined to investigate the claims of Jesus was because of what I saw in some Christians' lives. They did seem to have a friendliness, openness and integrity that was attractive.

Charles Bradlaugh was a Victorian atheist who opposed Christianity. One day, he challenged a Christian minister to hold a debate, comparing the claims of Christianity with those of atheism. The minister, Hugh Price Hughes, agreed to the challenge on one condition – that Mr Bradlaugh bring with him a hundred people whose lives had been changed for the better by their commitment to atheism. If he did so, Mr Hughes would also bring along a hundred people whose lives had changed through knowing Jesus. Knowing that Mr Bradlaugh could not fulfil this demand, he offered to drop the number to first fifty, then twenty, then ten and finally one! Understandably, Mr Bradlaugh had to withdraw his invitation. He could not produce one man or woman in whom his beliefs had brought about a real change of character for the better. Atheism has no moral power to change lives, whereas Jesus is continually doing this.

*"How can someone who lived
two thousand years ago
affect the way I live today?"*

Chapter 5

JESUS CAME TO DIE

Having looked at the evidence, we must tackle the next major question: "What was the purpose of Jesus' coming?"

Was it to demonstrate the sort of life we must live?

Some have supposed that the primary reason for Jesus' coming was to show us what real love is and demonstrate how God expects us to live. They would see Jesus' character as the most significant aspect of his life. Tennyson said, "His character was more wonderful than the greatest miracle." It certainly was remarkable and rightly his whole life compels our interest. Such people however would summarise Christian teaching as simply a code of behaviour to live by, much as other religions have their codes. This is not what the Bible teaches. Jesus' life has set us impossibly high standards. To the honest person, a study of his life will contrast starkly with our own, and will emphasise our inadequacy and even increase our guilt and hopelessness. Jesus came because he loves us. He does not want us to feel condemned by God but came instead to rescue us from the peril we are in. The answer in the Bible couldn't be clearer:

> For God did not send his Son into the world
> to condemn the world, but to save the world
> through him.
>
> *(John 3:17)*

Jesus came to rescue us

The Good News focuses not on what we have to do to please God, but on what Christ has done for us. Jesus came to **save** us, to make us secure, by having a relationship with God, even though we have not lived as we ought. He came to pay the price for our pardon, so giving us security and safety. The English word "safe" comes from the Latin *salvus* and from the same root come our words "save" and "salvation". Consequently, to be "saved" in the Christian sense simply means to be safe and secure with God.

What a claim – to save the world – to save us and to make us safe! We may not take to religion but is not this security and purpose just what many are really wanting in life?

The remarkable teaching of Jesus, his exemplary

character, and his miraculous healings made him stand out, yet he said that his death was to be the most significant part of his life. Whereas most biographers spend only a page or two on their hero's death, the gospel writers thought it so important that they devoted considerable space to the last week of his life. Matthew, Mark and Luke each devoted three whole chapters to his death, and John gives it no less than nine chapters out of a total of twenty-one. This is deliberate, not a sign that the books needed better editors to balance the layout! Jesus also understood his death to be the focus of his life.

> From that time on Jesus began to explain to his disciples that he **must** go to Jerusalem and suffer many things at the hands of the elders, chief priests and teachers of the law, and that he **must** be killed and on the third day be raised to life.
> *(Matthew 16:21, emphasis added)*

Some people maintain that if only Jesus could have lived to a ripe old age instead of dying between thirty-three and thirty-five, he might have made a bigger impact on the world and we would not be in the mess that we are today. On the contrary, the death of Jesus, his son, was the crucial point of God's plan, not a careless mistake.

Jesus told his twelve disciples, who became his apostles, and the apostles taught the world the stupendous fact that his death was the reason for his life; his teaching, his healing, his miracles and his character were all building up to and supporting this great climax. The death of Jesus was the reason he came to earth. That was the impact that set off the shock-waves that are still reverberating round the world nearly two thousand years later.

What was the purpose of his death? The apostle Peter summarises Jesus' answer:

> He himself bore our sins in his body on the tree, so that we might die to sins and live for righteousness; by his wounds you have been healed.
>
> *(1 Peter 2:24)*

Let us sort out what this means.

What is sin?

For many, "sin" is a religious concept with little practical significance.

There was a lady in my ward who had breast cancer. She queried why this had happened to her; "I've never done anyone any harm!" she exclaimed.

What rubbish! Of course she had – we all have. It is inherent in our nature. Those we dislike we try to put down. We lie to protect or elevate our own reputations. We steal to benefit ourselves. We are jealous of others' belongings or reputations. We constantly wound others with our words, either carelessly or deliberately.

Dr C. E. M. Joad was a colourful philosopher who regularly appeared on the BBC radio *Brains Trust* panel. For many years he had an optimistic view of human nature. It took World War II to shatter this. "Evil is endemic in man," he then concluded.

In practice we all know the reality of sin. We find it very attractive, extraordinarily so. Yet when we take that path we suffer the consequences. The pop group U2 sang,

"Sweet the sin, but bitter the taste in my mouth." Would any of us be happy to have a video of all our thoughts and actions shown publicly to those who know us? Not only would we see the bad things we do, the good we fail to do would also be seen. We all know that we stand guilty before God, who sees everything.

Some have tried to explain away this feeling of guilt by attributing it to a psychological aberration! Anne Russell wrote the poem, *Someone Else's Fault*.

> I went to my psychiatrist
> To be psychoanalysed,
> To find out why I killed the cat
> And blacked my husband's eyes.
>
> He laid me on a couch,
> To see what he could find.
> And here is what he dredged up,
> From my unconscious mind.
>
> When I was one my Mummy
> Hid my dolly in a trunk,
> And so it follows naturally
> That I am always drunk.
>
> When I was two I saw my Father
> Kiss the maid one day,
> And that is why I suffer from
> Kleptomania.
>
> When I was three I had the feeling
> Of ambivalence towards my brothers,

And so it follows naturally
I poisoned all my lovers.

But I am happy, now I've learnt
The lesson this has taught –
That everything that I do wrong
Is someone else's fault!

Others have tried to blame an external devil for their problems and so excuse themselves from responsibility. A theological student, training for ordination, gave it all up before completing the course. A little later he turned to crime but eventually was convicted of robbing a Post Office. Before passing sentence at his trial, the judge asked if the man had anything to say.

"Yes, my lord. I do not know what came over me. It must have been the devil who got into me."

The judge, who did know his Bible, immediately replied, "You should have learnt at college 'It is out of the heart of man that comes forth wickedness' – six years!"

God has told us how he wants us to live so that we can be contented, and at peace both with ourselves and with others around us. We fail at this, just as we fail in our relationship with God. It is our responsibility.

Why do we break God's rules?

We simply cannot help it. In the game of bowls a bowling wood has an inbuilt bias so that even if it starts off straight it naturally deviates away. We are like this. Even if we want to do what is right, we cannot – and, much of the time, we don't even want to do what is right.

> We all, like sheep, have gone astray, each of
> us has turned to his own way.
>
> *(Isaiah 53:6)*

We see life as revolving around ourselves: I want . . .
I like . . . I think . . . I am in the centre . . . Even the
spelling of the word "sin" is descriptive – 'I' in the centre.

Archbishop Temple said, "My original sin is that I put
myself in the centre of the picture, but I don't belong there
– God does."

In George Bernard Shaw's play *The Doctor's
Dilemma*, the doctor is described as "A self-made man
who worships his creator" (that means himself!). This is
the essence of sin.

God knows everything we have done, even those
wrong thoughts that we imagined were well hidden. Our
sin is the barrier between us and God. The prophet Isaiah
put it this way: "Your iniquities have separated you from
your God" (Isaiah 59:2).

This is the plight of all human beings – this separation
from God. Some people, in an effort to overcome it,
become religious: they go to church several times every
week; they give money to good causes; they read books
about their faith; they are actively good neighbours, and
they do the shopping for frail old ladies. But the fact
remains that there is nothing a person can do to make
himself or herself right with God! " . . . for all have sinned
and fall short of the Glory of God" (Romans 3:23).

There is nothing **we** can do to get rid of our sin. It
does not matter what religion a person has; even if he
belongs to the most doctrinally correct church, he would
still be in the same state. Just try and think for a moment
of being as good as God – the mind boggles – of course

it is impossible. No one is good – except God alone"
(Mark 10:18).

Yet this is the standard we need to attain to if we are to
enjoy and exist in God's company. "Your eyes are too
pure to look on evil; you cannot tolerate wrong"
(Habakkuk 1:13).

Written on the entrance to the temple of Apollo at
Delphi in ancient Greece was the motto "Know Thyself".
This is a good starting point – a recognition as to just
how sinful we are.

The solution

Not one of us can do a thing about this situation. But,
thank God, Jesus has. This is the good news. The word
"gospel" is derived from the old English word "Godspel"
which does literally mean "good news".

Jesus said that he came to earth from God in order to
provide an answer to this otherwise impossible dilemma.
He, God himself, would come and take the penalty and
effect of sin on himself. He, the one perfect man, would
become like the world's greatest murderer, thief, adulterer,
rapist, extortionist and liar, taking our faults on himself,
and would give us his status, his righteousness. "God
made him who had no sin to be sin for us" (2 Corinthians
5:21).

Stupendous, staggering good news.

This is the reason why the death of Jesus on the Cross
is so important. It was then that God took my sin on
himself. One of the great Bible verses says that Jesus came
'to give his life as a ransom for many' (Mark 10:45). We
are naturally slaves to sin, but Jesus has paid the price to
buy our freedom. He bore my sins in his body on the

Cross; by his wounds I have been healed!

If you consider some of the perplexing words that Jesus spoke during the time that he was dying on the Cross, it will make the picture of what he was doing clearer:

> "Father, forgive them for they do not know what they are doing."
>
> *(Luke 23:34)*

They did not understand that they were crucifying God himself. He then said:

> "My God, my God, why have you forsaken me?"
>
> *(Matthew 27:46)*

Now Jesus was the son of God; he was equal with God, so why was he forsaken (what a desperate, heart-rending word) by God? Jesus, on that Cross, became sin; and, being sin, he was necessarily separated from God exactly as my sins separate me from God.

"It is finished" (John 19:30) were among the last words he spoke before dying. In the original Greek of the gospel, the word used is *tetelestai* which is a commercial word meaning – "the debt is paid". When you complete the purchase of a car (or a camel), or pay a carpenter, "Paid in Full" is written on the bottom of the bill. In those days, he would have written *tetelestai* – the account is cleared, the job is done. Jesus has completed what he came to do.

Jesus says, "The account is cleared; I have taken your sins in my body on the Cross and by my wounds you have been healed", and that is the only way that we are able to become Christians – Christ's people – members of the family of God – close to God our Father. It is the most damnable and pernicious heresy (and I use those words very carefully) that has ever plagued the mind of man, that we can somehow make ourselves good enough to deserve to live with an almighty, all-holy God. It is outrageous for me to think that by trying to be good, trying to be religious and godly, I can make myself good enough to reach God.

When you die – and death is one of the facts that we all face – what will you say in order to gain entrance to God's presence? Will you say, "I've done my best" or "I've never done anyone any harm", (but God knows that's not true!) or "I've gone to church", or some other assertion that puts "I" first?

Such answers will be useless. The only valid answer will be that Jesus Christ has gained my right of admission for me.

Today, some say that the answers to the world's deepest problems lie with politics or technological advances. Jesus says he is the answer. Sir Richard Gregory was at one time editor of the scientific magazine *Nature*. He wrote his own epitaph:

> My grandfather preached the gospel of
> > Christ
> My father preached the gospel of
> > socialism
> I preach the gospel of science.

Which of these creeds ultimately helps people live at peace with God, their neighbours and themselves?
I am deeply and fully convinced that Jesus is God; that,

because of his love, he died for me on the Cross; and that there my many sins were dealt with. He has done that for me, so I long to live for him – and when I die I expect to continue in his glorious presence because Jesus has made it possible for me to do so. I make no apology for repeating Peter's astonishing words yet again: He himself bore our sins in his body on the tree, so that we might die to sins and live for righteousness; by his wounds you have been healed" (1 Peter 2:24).

Sawat was a young Thai, who left his village for the high life of the capital, Bangkok. He met up with a bad group, began to sell opium, and became involved with organised prostitution. Finally, he began to buy and sell young girls. He became a central figure in these sordid trades, much to the disgrace of his godly father. Then disaster struck. He was robbed, arrested, and lost all his wealth, friends and status, ending up living in a dilapidated shack by the city rubbish heap. Then he thought again of his father, a simple Christian man, whose parting words had been, "I will be waiting for you." Sawat wondered if, after all these years and the disgrace he had caused, he would be welcome back home. So he wrote, "Dear Father, I want to come home, but I don't know if you will receive me after all that I have done. I have sinned greatly. Please forgive me. On Saturday night, I will be on the train which goes through our village. If you are still waiting for me, will you tie a piece of cloth on the *po* tree in front of our house."

That train journey was horrible for Sawat. He kept thinking about the evil life he had led and was afraid of possible rejection. Sitting opposite him in the train was a complete stranger who noticed Sawat's nervousness. Eventually, the whole story came out. As they approached the village, Sawat could take no more. "Oh sir, I cannot bear to look. Can you watch for me?", and he buried his face in his knees.

"Do you see it sir? It is the only house with a *po* tree."

"Young man," said the stranger, looking out of the window, "Your father did not hang one piece – look! He has covered the whole tree with pieces of cloth." As Sawat looked, he saw that in his front yard was his father, dancing up and down waving yet another white cloth. He ran beside the slow moving train and, when Sawat alighted, he threw his arms around him and, with tears of joy in his eyes, said, "I've been waiting for you." Such is the love God has for us; he wants all people to come to him and enter into his family.

Now everyone can approach God

So God is now approachable – directly approachable, without any intermediary – by anyone in the world. In spite of the fact that we in the churches seem to have got into our heads that the Christian gospel is only for religious people, Christ taught that he had come for **everyone** and particularly for the outsiders, the non-religious.

"Go and make disciples of all nations", he said, (Matthew 28:19) so that all of us might have the opportunity to become the sons of God, whatever our upbringing. Jews and Muslims have impersonal and distant names for God; the Christian's name for God is "Father".

I once saw a short play that was set at the gates of heaven. Two angels walked onto the stage: one a rather stiff being in uniform, and the other an attractive female angel. They had been told to expect newcomers to heaven.

At this point, a ruffian slouched onto the stage.

"Is this the place?" he asked roughly.

"This is the gate of heaven," the formal angel replied in a rather superior voice.

"Oh good, that's what I want."

The guardian angel eyed him suspiciously, obviously doubting his credentials for admission to heaven. So he quizzed him as to his eligibility. "Are you one of the 'chosen brethren' sir?"

"What?" the man replied.

"I mean – have you been 'redeemed by the blood' sir?"

"What are you going on about?"

The haughty angel's doubts seemed confirmed. "Are you sure you are in the right place, sir?"

"Oh yeah. You see, I was told to be here. It all started when me and me mate was doing a job – but we was caught because he chose the wrong house. It was the Roman governor's we robbed. We was arrested and then condemned to death by crucifixion. Very nasty. But the man, if he is just a man, who died next to me wasn't in the same league as us, and he told me, 'This day you will be with me in paradise'."

This story is a strong reminder that it is not just the nice respectable people that God loves and wants to be his people; it is all of us.

Now when God looks at his people, he does not see the good that we have done – this is inadequate to satisfy God. What he sees is the status of perfection that Jesus has given us by dying for us on the Cross. He has taken away my sins and I, even I, am now completely free (and this is almost incredible) to approach the Almighty himself and to say with the once doubting Thomas: "My Lord and my God" (John 20:28).

A vicar, wearing a dog-collar, was walking out of his church when he met a rather uncouth Irish man lurching by with a week's growth on his chin and a bottle of spirits in his pocket. "Say one for us, Father," he asked. The vicar, who was a godly man, shot back, "Say one for yourself, you lazy coot!" but he did go on to explain that now everyone can approach God directly and speak to him as a son speaks to a loved and trusted father.

And that is the joyous truth: that, even if we have never gone to church, even if we swear, lie, steal, torment or even have murdered, we now have the means to approach God.

This reassuring, inspiring news is relevant to everyone, whatever state they are in. One day, I was sitting on the edge of a patient's bed; she was very tired and weak and obviously dying, but suddenly she perked up and asked, "Mr Palmer, how long is it before I go home?"

"Well, I'm not sure that you would be able to manage by yourself at home", I replied. She smiled, "No, I don't mean that, I mean my home in heaven – to be with Jesus." Her trust in Jesus had left no room at all for fear in her mind. This sense of security is what God wants us all to have.

*"Of course I am a Christian!
I'm a good person and I
don't rob or steal . . . I live
a Christian life."*

Chapter 6

WHO IS A CHRISTIAN?

How few people stop to ask this vital question. If they do, all too often they make up their own answer. This chapter will look at who Jesus says is acceptable to him.

When people are admitted to hospital, one question they are always asked is to state their religion. Most put down "C of E". For many, however, this seems to mean "Confused of England".

Perhaps you have seen the car sticker that says: "Don't stop me, I'm too busy trying to get there, But I don't know where!"

Many people rush through life without thinking where they are going and whether they are on the right track.

Having a full life – whether because of children, overwork, sport or other activities – can fill our time, but all these things fail to satisfy in the end. As Albert Camus, the philosopher, said, "What is intolerable is to see one's life drained of meaning."

In a recent radio programme, 80% claimed that they believed in God, yet one third cannot remember the last time they read a part of the Bible, and five out of six never attend church. This is unconscious atheism. People have not deliberately renounced a belief in God in the same way as they have renounced churches, but they behave as if God is not relevant – as if he were an optional extra for those who have a need!

The Bible certainly teaches that to be a Christian demands an active involvement with Jesus. There is no such thing as a passive Christian. Just because a person is brought up in a Christian family or country does not make him a Christian. Even baptism or confirmation is not a guarantee that someone is acceptable to God.

Religion is not the answer!

Ever since the beginning of civilisation, people have felt that God was approachable by means of religious ceremonies or practices. Jesus taught that this is not correct. The Sermon on the Mount was the first training programme that Jesus held for his disciples. One of the major topics he deals with from beginning to end is, "Who is acceptable to God?" At one point, he describes what will happen at the final judgement when all of us will come face to face with Jesus Christ. He said:

"Not everyone who says to me, 'Lord, Lord,'

will enter the kingdom of heaven, but only
he who does the will of my father who is in
heaven. Many will say to me on that day,
'Lord, Lord, did we not prophesy in your
name, and in your name drive out demons
and perform many miracles?' Then I will
tell them plainly, 'I never knew you. Away
from me, you evildoers!"
(Matthew 7:21–3)

This is tough teaching, certainly not a candy-floss
Christianity! Note that many people who recognise Jesus
and even refer to him as "Lord" are not acceptable to
him. Jesus is very clear that being a churchgoer, or even
a church leader, or a person who has a supernatural gift,
is not a guarantee of our acceptance. Those who are
acceptable to God are those who are inwardly committed
to doing what God wants. Such people have a special
relationship with him and are personally known by him.

Outward appearances can be deceptive. When we look
at other people's lives, we tend to grade them into shades
of grey. Those who appear to be good and kind, such as
the Mother Teresas of this world, are light grey. Those
who appear to be particularly evil, we paint as dark grey.
We usually place ourselves somewhere near the middle
with our neighbours, and work-mates always a slightly
darker shade of grey below us!

God, however, does not classify us on this basis – he
only recognises two groups of people: the totally black
spiritually (those who do not belong to him), and the pure
white (those who are his and have been totally forgiven).
The Bible teaches that each of us is either in the "light"
or in "darkness," – we are either "sheep" or "goats" (there

are no "shoats"); either "wheat" or "tares". Jesus clearly teaches that either we are Christians, who are recognised and known by God, or we are not part of his kingdom!

One Sunday evening, a vicar overheard his son praying. The boy said, "Please help the faith of daddy to drop a foot." The following morning, the vicar asked his son to explain his prayer. "We learnt in Sunday School yesterday," the lad replied, "that you can have two sorts of faith: one in your head only, the other in your heart." Academic belief is not what God requires. He wants us to understand how much he loves us and what he has done to enable us to be forgiven. A real grasp of this will inevitably lead to a commitment of my whole being to live with and for my God.

What makes a person a Christian?

The answer to this question is vital. We have already seen that being religious does not make us Christians.

When John Bunyan was in Bedford prison for twelve years for refusing not to teach others the Christian gospel, he used to write little poems that he named "Divine Emblems". One of them went:

> An egg's no chick by falling from the hen,
> Nor man a Christian till he's born again!

This phrase "born again" has been bandied about without much understanding. It appears that American politicians have to use this title to describe themselves in order to have a chance of being elected. It was first used, however, by Jesus when a good, fervent Jewish leader approached Jesus one night to learn more about who Jesus was. Jesus startled him by saying: "I tell you the truth, no one can see the kingdom of God unless he is born again" (John 3:3).

Jesus then explained that he was not speaking physically but spiritually. A new beginning had to be made. Just as we cannot bring about our own natural birth, so our spiritual birth must come "from above". It is something God gives us if we really want it.

At the start of his preaching ministry:

> . . . Jesus went into Galilee, proclaiming the good news of God. "The time has come," he said. "The kingdom of God is near. Repent and believe the good news!"
>
> *(Mark 1:15)*

The kingdom of God consists of those people who acknowledge the king, and Jesus taught that this will involve three things. Just as a three-legged stool is useless without all three legs, so we absorb these three items if we are to become Christians.

1. Repentance – one Lord

This is a key word but it is poorly understood by many people. It means much more than just saying "Sorry, I did wrong." The original Greek word is *metanoia*. *Meta* means "change", and *noia* means "mind" – so *metanoia* means a "change of mind". Thus the word really means "having a complete change of heart and mind". It involves making a new start with a change of direction in your life, turning right away from living for yourself to living for and with Jesus. This change of direction is a vital pre-requisite if God is to accept anyone as one of his people. Obviously, none of us is able to do exactly what our heavenly Father wants all the time, since we are not perfect, but it is that commitment to him that is so important. It will show itself when we do fail. In a marriage, it is important whenever something goes wrong, perhaps an argument, that people learn to make up and say sorry quickly. So it is with God. Repentance means that we have started on a new path and so, whenever we deviate from it, we must return to the right road.

This major requirement to repent is a constant theme throughout the Bible. The Old Testament prophets and John the Baptist made it a major topic of their preaching. When the apostle Peter gave his first sermon to the crowds in Jerusalem seven weeks after the crucifixion of Jesus, he told them who Jesus really was – God in the flesh, the promised Jewish Messiah, who had been raised from the dead by God to prove this claim. Many of his listeners were cut to the heart. "What shall we do?" they asked. Peter replied, "Repent and be baptised, every one of you, in the name of Jesus Christ for the forgiveness of your sins" (Acts 2:38).

The message has always been the same. "You will be my people and I will be your God" (Ezekiel 36:28). With these words the prophet Ezekiel summarised the relationship God wants to have with us. The binding covenant, like a marriage, is one in which God promises to love, forgive, protect and motivate us, as we allow him into the driving seat of our lives. God has kept his side of the covenant – he is our God who gives us all that we need and more – but what about our response? Much of the Old Testament is a painful reminder of the thousand and one ways in which people disobey, ignore, rewrite and otherwise fail to take up our side of the covenant.

Any individual who wants to be forgiven by God **must** change the direction of their lives, to have Jesus as their Lord. Our Father offers his love and forgiveness to every single one of us, and longs for us to accept and become involved with him, but (and this is an important point) he does not force himself on us. We are perfectly free to refuse his offer, and just turn our backs. Most of us do just that – politely of course! If, however, we really want this gift, we have to take it. At the beginning of John's gospel is the sad reminder that the Messiah came to the Jews, God's people, but many of them rejected him. Now it is wide open for anyone, whatever our colour or race, to become one of his special people, one of his family.

> He came to that which was his own, but his own did not receive him. Yet to all who received him, to those who believed in his name, he gave the right to become children of God – children born not of natural descent, nor of human decision or a husband's will, but born of God.
> *(John 1:11–13)*

It is amazing how many people naively say that they like the teaching of the Sermon on the Mount, but don't like doctrine or theology. They can never have read it if they suppose it is just saying, "Be kind, be good." In this sermon, Jesus gives a powerful illustration about two roads:

> Enter through the narrow gate. For wide is the gate and broad is the road that leads to

destruction, and many enter through it. But
small is the gate and narrow the road that
leads to life, and only a few find it."

(Matthew 7:13–14)

You can imagine the travellers casually strolling down
this wide, easy road, happily chatting with their friends,
but not knowing where they are heading. Jesus teaches
that this wide road leads to a place called "destruction"
or "hell". There is another road, however, that turns off
the broad road. This is narrow, goes uphill and the going
is far from easy – but its destination is "life" or "heaven".
There are few people on this narrow road; the majority
are still on the broad road. Jesus is at the division of the
roads and is urging people to turn off the broad way and
join him on the journey along the new path. A good name
for the gate at the beginning of this path would be the
"Gate of Repentance".

It is sobering to realise that, out of all the population
of the world, only a few will turn through the "Gate of
Repentance" and climb the narrow road to the rewards at
the end. Most people rush past without noticing it, or, if
they do see it, they think the way looks too difficult; but
what is the use of taking the easy way if it does not lead
to the destination you want to reach?

Martin Luther, the sixteenth-century reformer, stressed
that Christianity needs personal pronouns. Many people
say "Jesus is Lord", but the Christian can say "Jesus is
my Lord." A faith that has not begun with my personally
turning to God has not yet begun!

2. One faith

Many sects and denominations have different

emphases and sometimes diametrically opposed views that cannot all be what God wants. Primarily, a Christian is committed to obeying the teaching of Jesus. This is why the apostles took so much effort in carefully recording what Jesus did, taught and meant, so that there should be no confusion over what God's truth is.

There are some people who say, "Yes, I am doing God's will – but I am doing it in my way." At the end of the Sermon on the Mount, Jesus defines more precisely what it means to "do God's will". He tells the parable of the wise and foolish men who set out to build houses – the houses of their lives. The wise man built his house on the rock and, when the storms of life came (and the greatest of these will be the final judgement before God), he stood firm. The foolish man built a house looking very similar, but he only had sand as his foundation. For a while, they would have looked just the same, until the storms and floods arrived! The key question is, "What does it mean to build your house on the rock?" Jesus answers this clearly: "Therefore everyone who hears these words of mine and puts them into practice is like a wise man who built his house on the rock" (Matthew 7:24).

The rock is obedience to what Jesus taught. To obey God is to obey Jesus; to disobey Jesus is to disobey God. Hence it is nonsense to say, "I serve God in my own way"; that is not sufficient.

It is not surprising that the vast majority of growing churches are ones where the central concern is to teach and explain the Bible. There is only one faith – that of Jesus. The apostles taught what Jesus taught. That is why the church is called "apostolic" – it holds to the original apostolic teaching. St Paul summarised this view of the Bible when he wrote: "All Scripture is God-breathed and is useful for teaching, rebuking, correcting and training in righteousness, so that the man of God may be thoroughly equipped for every good work" (2 Timothy 3:16–17).

St Columba, who left Ireland in the mid-sixth century to teach the Scottish people about Jesus, said, "The Holy Scriptures are the only rule of faith."

John Wycliffe, the fourteenth-century church leader from Oxford, said:

> Holy Scripture is the faultless, most true, most perfect and most holy law of God, which it is the duty of all men to learn, to know, to defend and to observe, inasmuch as they are bound to serve the Lord in accordance with it, under the promise of an eternal reward.

It is these scriptures that teach that a person is not a Christian unless he has repented and is committed to living in obedience to the will of Jesus.

Christian faith is a trust and reliance in Jesus; obedience to what God has taught us in the Bible is the proof that we have faith.

3. One baptism

A Christian has personally responded to Christ's claims over him, but the Christian faith is essentially corporate and not solitary. Jesus came to establish a kingdom – a group of people who acknowledge him. When the listeners were challenged at Peter's first sermon after Pentecost they asked how they should respond to this message.

> Repent and be baptised, every one of you,
> in the name of Jesus Christ for the
> forgiveness of your sins. And you will
> receive the gift of the Holy Spirit.
>
> *(Acts 2:38)*

Personal repentance is essential, but so is a public acknowledgment of my change of direction. "In the name of Jesus Christ" means a very specific new allegiance to Jesus and his teaching; it is not just a baptism of repentance, although that is part of it. It would certainly not be easy for those Jews in Jerusalem to make a public acknowledgement of Jesus so soon after the authorities had executed him, but this was part of the threefold response God wants.

Baptism also symbolises that Jesus has completely washed away my sin, that the old life has gone and a new life with God and his people has begun.

It is said of Augustine, the fourth-century scholar who became the greatest theologian amongst the Church Fathers, that prior to his becoming a Christian he had had a few amorous flirtations! Soon after he opened his life to God he was walking down a street in Milan. He saw an old girl friend on the other side of the road, but decided not to stop but to walk on.

"Augi, it is me," the girl called out.

"But it is not me," Augustine replied.

Augustine was clear in his mind that he had started on a new path and did not want to get embroiled in the past.

This radical change is exactly what becoming a Christian means. St Paul wrote: "Therefore, if anyone is in Christ, he is a new creation; the old has gone, the new has come!" (2 Corinthians 5:17).

When Jesus gave his final orders to his disciples, he commanded: "Therefore go and make disciples out of all nations, baptising them in the name of the Father and of the Son and of the Holy Spirit, and teaching them to obey everything that I have commanded you" (Matthew 28:19–20).

People may be inclined to keep their new commitment secret, but this is not the will of God. Christ died publicly for us, and he wants our death to the old life to be public also.

There has been considerable confusion about the details of baptism. A Chinese Christian noted the varied practices of the different denominational missions in his country. Some baptised by immersion, others by sprinkling, and yet others not at all. He summarised these differences with the phrase, "Big wash, little wash and dry clean!" The important common denominator, however, was being made clean.

I was leading a student house party in Hungary when a local student came to see me, wanting to become a Christian. We went through what was involved, step by step. He understood that he had to repent of living for himself and change to having Jesus in charge. He understood that to live as a Christian involved obedience to the teaching of Jesus in the Bible. He then prayed a very moving prayer, asking Jesus to come into his life. However, when I reminded him that he now needed to let others know of his new allegiance, he could not face this; he had been notorious as a rebel student! All I could do was leave him with a verse written out on a card:

I tell you, whoever acknowledges me before men, the Son of Man will also acknowledge

him before the angels of God. But he who
disowns me before men will be disowned
before the angels of God.

(Luke 12:8–9)

Too hard?

This all sounds very daunting, and many will gulp at
the large commitment involved. "I'll never be able to
keep it up," they wistfully say. This is true! However, to
think like that is to leave out an essential part of the
equation. God has promised that all those who repent
and go public **will** receive the Holy Spirit into their lives.
He is the motivating force that will keep us going.

Peter replied, "Repent and be baptised, every
one of you, in the name of Jesus Christ for
the forgiveness of your sins. And you will
receive the gift of the Holy Spirit."

(Acts 2:38)

When people become Christians, they will quickly
notice the effect of the Holy Spirit. They will want to
meet up with other Christians, will have a hunger to know
and understand the Bible, want to pray, and their
consciences will become more acute. When a person turns
off the broad way on to the narrow way at the call of
Jesus, they find a new friend comes alongside them as
they travel along the new road – the Spirit of God himself.
He keeps us going, and, when we stumble, he helps us to
start up again.

When my youngest son, Andrew, was three years old,
we were walking down the main street of our town. He

put his small hand into mine. Suddenly, he saw something exciting on the other side of the busy road, and started to move off. It was then that he realised that, when he put his hand into mine, it was not just him holding on to me, but much more significant was the fact that I was holding him – securely. It is the same with God. We, perhaps hesitatingly, put ourselves into his hand. There may be doubts as to whether we will be able to keep up our new commitment, when temptations come our way. It is then that we will experience God's hold of us. We will meet people who will encourage us, and the Lord will stimulate our consciences, so that the most important relationship we can have, that with God, remains secure and warm.

In the third century, a man wrote to a friend:

> It is a bad world, Donatus, an incredibly bad world. But I've discovered in the midst of it a quiet and holy people who have learnt a great secret. They found a joy that is a thousand times better than any of the pleasures of our sinful life. They are despised and persecuted but they care not. They are masters of their souls, they have overcome the world. These people, Donatus, are Christians – and I am one of them.

This man had not only discovered the Christian story and believed it to be true, he also realised that he had to respond to the message.

*"Why do I
have to make a decision?"*

Chapter 7

CHANGE DIRECTION?

Many years ago, a man was condemned to death by hanging. There was considerable public agitation on his behalf. A few days before the execution, a message was received from the Home Office saying that a pardon had been granted. When the prison governor informed the condemned man of his reprieve, he was shocked by the reply, "I have finished with life – I do not want a pardon." The governor was perplexed and asked the Home Secretary what should be done. The answer came back, "A pardon that is not accepted is only a scrap of paper."

We must act and accept Christ's forgiveness that he won for us on the Cross, in order for it to be valid for us.

Joshua was the leader of the Jewish people after Moses

died. He was the man who led the Jews to capture the cities in the promised land. At the end of his life, Joshua summoned all the important Israelites to meet him at the city of Shechem. After recounting the stories of what God had done for his people, he challenged them: "Now fear the Lord and serve him with all faithfulness, . . . But if serving the Lord seems undesirable to you, then choose for yourselves this day whom you will serve" (Joshua 24:14–15).

All people must make this same decision. To make no decision is to carry on down the road we have been travelling on – down the broad way.

The Israelites replied to Joshua, "We will serve the Lord."

Sham Christians

There are many places in the Bible where Jesus condemns insincere commitment to God. Today, there is a vogue to praise anyone who has some sort of faith, whatever it is. Jesus was never so naive. He was interested in seeing that people follow God's wishes. Anything else, even if well intentioned, would not please God. Many of the teachers of the Law and Pharisees of Jesus' day were deeply committed in their religious beliefs. They took them very seriously indeed. Jesus, however, certainly did not think this devotion was good enough for God. He thought it was a man-orientated religion. "Everything they do is done for men to see" (Matthew 23:5).

Jesus hated hypocrisy and was willing to attack it openly. To the same group of religious people, he said: " . . . you hypocrites! You are like whitewashed tombs, which look beautiful on the outside but on the inside are full of dead men's bones and everything unclean. In the same way, on the outside you appear to people as righteous but on the inside you are full of hypocrisy and wickedness" (Matthew 23:27–8).

It is how we appear to God that matters!

I am particularly conscious of this because I was a sham Christian. I found church and school religion uninspiring to say the least. I had picked up enough theology to be able to give reasonable answers to straightforward questions – and so I looked on myself as a Christian, and put "C of E" on forms.

Then I went up to university and met a group of men whose commitment to Jesus was inspiring. They enjoyed the same sports as I did; they were fun to be with, and, although they belonged to various denominations, they all shared the same deep commitment to Christ. They used to take me to listen to sermons and talks and gradually it got through to me that I wasn't quite all that I should be – that in fact I was not really a Christian yet.

One day, a friend invited me to come to his room where an American named George Verwer was going to give a talk. I remember the evening vividly: it was a large room for a student and I sat on the floor at the back. He spoke on a verse from John's first epistle: "Let us not love with words or tongue but with actions and in truth" (1 John 3:18).

As he talked, I realised that my commitment to God was nothing but words, and the longer I listened, the more aware I became that God wanted it to be real.

Afterwards, I went back to my room and knelt down by my bed and fought a battle. I knew God wanted me to be his, but what would my other friends think of me? Should I really commit my life to God? Could I not defer this decision? One side of me knew that the Lord wanted me to be a Christian, but the other side kept thinking of reasons to wait. I would have to get involved with the "God Squad" – some might ridicule me.

The struggle lasted perhaps half an hour, but the pounding of God on my conscience won through. I prayed, "Lord, come into my life. Help me to be the sort of person you want me to be. I want to be your person. I need your forgiveness." That was it. There were no bright lights or ecstasy – just a simple relief that I knew I had done what was right. The following day, I told my friend what had happened, and he was overjoyed. He then gave me some very sound advice, "Go and do some studying and be absolutely certain that the Christian faith is true – really true – so that, when the pressures come, you will be able to keep going strongly."

Change direction

This commitment to "Repent" and "Follow the Lord" is vital. Towards the end of the first century, there was a church in the affluent city of Laodicea (in present-day Turkey). As so often happens, the church reflected the weaknesses of the society it was in. They believed the right doctrines and were consequently satisfied with themselves, but God found their affluent smugness literally nauseating. Their actions showed them to be only lukewarm in their allegiance to the Lord Jesus. God urged them to do something about this desperate situation. "So be earnest, and repent. Here I am! I stand at the door and knock. If anyone hears my voice and opens the door, I will come in and eat with him, and he with me" (Revelation 3:19–20).

Although this was said to a religious group, it can apply to anyone. We must all be in earnest; we cannot trifle about our relationship with God. Jesus demands to be accepted on his terms, and he will then give us not only the forgiveness we need to be able to stand before God, but also the thrill of his presence with us as we live for him.

In the early years of this century, Bishop Taylor Smith was preaching in a large English cathedral. He was emphasising this need of all people to make a new start with God on his terms. He told the story of the upright Jewish leader, Nicodemus, who came to meet Jesus one night and was told: "I tell you the truth, no one can enter the kingdom of God unless he is born of water and the Spirit. Flesh gives birth to flesh, but the Spirit gives birth to spirit. You should not be surprised at my saying, 'You must be born again' " (John 3:5–7).

The bishop continued, "Even that undoubtedly good man needed to turn towards his Saviour and make a fresh start, before he could become a subject of the kingdom of God – one of God's people. My dear people, do not substitute anything for the new birth. You may be a member of a church, but church membership is not new birth, for 'except a man be born again, he cannot see the Kingdom of God' ".

On his left sat the archdeacon in his stall, dressed in all his official robes. Pointing directly at him, the bishop said, "You may even be an archdeacon, like my friend in his stall, and not be 'born again', for 'except a man be born again he cannot see the kingdom of God'," and continued with his sermon.

A day or so later, the bishop received a note from the archdeacon: "You have found me out. I have been a clergyman for over thirty years but I have never known anything of the joy that Christians speak of. I never could understand. Mine has been a hard legal service. I did not know what the matter was with me, but, when you pointed directly at me – and said, 'You might even be an archdeacon and not be born again,' I realised in a moment what the trouble was. I had never known anything of the new birth."

You can imagine the delight of that bishop when they met up the following day and he was able to explain to the archdeacon the simple truths of what God has done for us and what he requires of us. It is not our attempts at righteousness nor our adherence to a code of behaviour that can make us right with God, but only our utter dependence on a Saviour. The archdeacon prayed and acknowledged his own need for a Saviour, and invited the Lord into his life to take charge.

The change

The change in our lives when we become Christians is radical. It is a disaster that many think that Christians don't do *this* and don't do *that* . . . and stop thinking. I have found the opposite is true – becoming a Christian has meant taking on new interests and activities that are infinitely worthwhile, and I began to think far more. True religion and reason should go 'hand in hand'.

When Augustine of Hippo became a Christian in 387 AD, his whole life changed in appreciation of what God had done for him. He described a Christian as 'a hallelujah from head to foot'. He wrote 'Let me not tire of thanking you for your mercy in rescuing me from all my wicked ways'. He never stopped using his mind and affirmed,

'Christians think in believing and believe in thinking!'

One of the early changes in me was a longing to understand the Bible. I joined a Bible study group. At first this was daunting and embarrassing as everyone else seemed to know far more than I did, but it didn't take long before I felt at home. There were so many questions! I wanted to be certain that in the Bible we have 'the very words of God' (Romans 3:2) and I am now convinced of this. This desire to understand the Bible better has never left me. My prime motive for studying the Bible now is to learn how God thinks and to begin to think similarly and consequently behave in a way that pleases him. Godly thinking produces godly lives, whereas sloppy doctrine produces sloppy lives.

So I am really grateful that I became involved with churches that emphasised the importance of the Bible. What a privilege it was to be taught it by men of the calibre of David Watson, who was then a curate at the Round Church in Cambridge, and Dick Lucas of St. Helen's Church, Bishopsgate, who had such an obvious love for the Lord. As a surgeon it is very easy to be arrogant, overbearing and self-centred. Yet to know, from the Bible, that all I am and have is from God, and that one day I will have to give an account to my Saviour on the way I have lived, must have an effect on my lifestyle!

As the friendship with my Lord deepened, I found my conscience became more acute. My overriding concern has changed from doing what would be socially popular, to doing what pleases God. Such tensions are not always easy to deal with, and it does mean that I need to discuss any decisions or problems with my Lord in prayer. It really is thrilling to discover that He does care and longs to be involved in every aspect of my life.

It did not take long before I began to want my friends to understand that Jesus really is the creator of the Universe, and that He has the answers to all those questions that begin with 'why'. I began to invite others to come and hear the sort of Christian talks I had been taken along to. I wanted them to see that Jesus could satisfy all people, intellectuals included, and that there didn't have to be a 'cringe factor' at Christian meetings. I still cannot understand why some church leaders make the proclamation of such a thrilling story so embarrassing, when it is true and relevant to everyone.

I have now come to learn that there is a real satisfaction in living with Jesus that cannot be matched by other ambitions. What I find remarkable is that I now want, deep down, to do what pleases him. I still have questions, and all too often I fail to live in a way that pleases him, but the desire is still there. Many years ago God promised that this is exactly what he would do.

> I will give you a new heart and put a new spirit in you . . . I will put my Spirit in you and move you to follow my decrees and be careful to keep my laws.
>
> *(Ezekiel 36:26–27)*

Chapter 8

CROSSROADS

Sacred Hearts was a film about some girls living in a Roman Catholic orphanage during the last war. One of the girls admitted to the rather austere nun in charge that she had lost her faith, with the words:

"I have lost my faith; I just started to think and I lost my faith."

To this, the nun replied:

"Well, stop thinking and your faith will come back."

It should be the very opposite. Think clearly, look at and weigh up all the evidence and you will see that the Christian story is true.

1. Jesus really did exist and claim to be God, the Saviour of the world.

2.   He did do remarkable miracles – even
      his opponents agreed to that.

3.   He did rise again from the dead – and
      his disciples gave their lives
      confirming this.

4.   The Old Testament prophecies
      accurately predict that Jesus is God's
      Messiah and these could not be
      fulfilled by anyone else.

5.   When we listen to what Jesus taught,
      it does have "that ring of truth".

Why cannot everyone see this? Some years ago, a
man was standing on a soap box at Hyde Park Corner,
trying to ridicule the Christian message. "People tell me
God exists, but I cannot see him. People tell me that that
there is life after death – but I cannot see it. People tell
me there is a judgement to come – but I cannot see it.
People tell me there is a heaven and a hell – but I can't
see them."

There was a slight ripple of applause as he climbed
down. Another man then struggled up on to the soap box
and said, "People tell me there is green grass around –
but I cannot see it. People tell me there is a blue sky
above but I cannot see it. People tell me there are
trees nearby but I cannot see them; it is because I am
blind!"

This is the diagnosis that the Bible makes. "The god
of this age has blinded the minds of unbelievers, so that

they cannot see the light of the gospel of the glory of Christ, who is the image of God" (2 Corinthians 4:4).

Several years ago, I was discussing the claims of Jesus Christ with a medical student. We spent some time looking at the evidence for the Christian faith. He seemed to agree with nearly all the points made, so I asked him whether he would like to become a Christian. He replied:

"No, you see – I don't want to."

Effects of denying God

All too often, the reasons that people give for rejecting Christ are superficially intellectual – but nearly always the real reason is moral: we want to be in charge of our lives and live for ourselves. The agnostic author, Aldous Huxley, when he was an elderly man, admitted that he had such biases when rejecting Christianity when he was young.

> I had motives for not wanting the world to have a meaning – consequently assumed that it had none, and was able without any difficulty to find satisfying reasons for this assumption. For myself, the philosophy of meaninglessness was essentially an instrument of liberation, sexual and political.

The interesting fact is that all people have their religion. If, for their own reasons, they reject God, they will always put a substitute in his place, and it is remarkable how much time, energy and commitment is spent on these gods. For some, the god is the pursuit of wealth; for others, power, and yet for others it is self-satisfaction. All too often, these gods prevent people thinking clearly about why and for what purpose they are here. There will be unfortunate side-effects when people put themselves in God's place. In their marriages, they will put themselves first – so it will not be surprising if the divorce rate goes up rapidly. Sexual gratification will become a prime goal, so the number of unwanted pregnancies, abortions, and sexually transmitted diseases (such as AIDS and cancer of the cervix) will increase. There will also be much more unbearable stress, as people find that living in ways that God did not design us for is not as ideal as they dreamed. **Integrity** will begin to disappear. Few realise that the opposite of integrity is **disintegrity** – or, put in more common language, **disintegration**! When a person loses his integrity, when he ceases to live for what is right, then his personal life, his family life, his social life and eventually the nation's life will begin to disintegrate. This is one of the main lessons we can learn from history!

There is another disastrous consequence of denying the existence of God. There remains no rational reason why all people must be honest, kind or loving. We would then only be a chance conglomeration of meaningless atoms! Jean-Paul Sartre wrote in 1946:

> The existentialist finds it extremely embarrassing that God does not exist – for there disappears with him all possibility of finding moral values in an intelligible universe.

Take a step

In spite of all this evidence, it may not be easy to put my trust in Jesus. Sheldon Vanauken was a student of English literature, first at Yale University and then at Oxford, where he met the Christian writer C. S. Lewis. He began to look at the claims of Jesus and, the more he looked, the more probable it seemed. However hard he looked, there still remained a gap between the probable and the proved. He did not know how to bridge that gap and make a "step of faith." He wrote this:

> There is a gap between the probable and the proved. How was I to cross it? If I were to stake my whole life on the risen Christ, I wanted proof – I wanted certainty. I wanted to see him eat a bit of fish. I wanted letters of fire across the sky. I got none of these. And I continued to hang about on the edge of the gap ... it was a question of whether I was going to accept him or reject him.
>
> My God, there was a gap behind me as well. Perhaps the leap to acceptance was a horrifying gamble, but what of the leap to rejection!
>
> There might be no absolute certainty that Christ was God, but by God there was no certainty that he was not. This was not to be borne. I could not reject Jesus. There was only one thing to do once I had seen the gap behind me. I turned away from it, and flung myself over the gap towards Jesus.

When a person realises how much they fall short of what God requires, how much they need to be forgiven, how much evidence there is that Jesus is the Saviour of the world, they must regard the Christian faith as probable. When he or she then sees how great the moral, intellectual and philosophical vacuum there is without him, then the impetus to take that step of allegiance to Jesus is immense.

Some people may say, "Yes, I agree – I am just waiting for something to happen." There is a Chinese proverb which says, "Man stand long time with mouth wide open waiting for roast duck to fly in."

We must act! Not to make a decision about the place Jesus will have in your life is tantamount to rejecting him.

Eventually, each one of us will stand before God – and what we have done with our lives will be revealed. No one will be able to feel satisfied in his presence. The Bible teaches that a special book will then be opened that contains the names of all those to whom Jesus has given eternal life as a free gift, who have turned to him during this life and sought his forgiveness. Those whose names are in that book will be allowed to join their Saviour in heaven. If a person's name is not found in that book, they will be thrown out of God's presence (Revelation 20:11–15). The stakes are high!

Some treat these matters as a trifling business, being ignorant of the seriousness of their position. God, however, cannot be trifled with. He is not just suggesting that we might be happier with him. He, the Creator of the Universe, who came to this earth to give us all a chance, **commands** that we take him seriously.

When the apostle Paul first preached the Christian gospel in Athens, he was not overawed by the intellects

of those listening, but finished his sermon with the words:
" . . . But now he commands all people everywhere to
repent. For he has set a day when he will judge the world
with justice by the man he has appointed. He has given
proof of this to all men by raising him from the dead"
(Acts 17:30–31).

After this talk, some sneered; others wanted to know
more, and a few opened their lives to Jesus Christ. This
will be the reaction wherever the gospel is told.

How not to respond?

A few years ago on a Sunday evening, a young
communist wandered into a City of London church.
During Evensong the visitor was deeply struck by the
words of the *Magnificat*. This is the song of Mary when
she was pregnant with Jesus, and includes the words: "He
has filled the hungry with good things but has sent the
rich away empty" (Luke 1:53).

This sounded interesting. He had never been told that
Jesus was interested in the underprivileged. So, after the
service, he went up to the minister and explained how he
had been moved by the words of the service.

"What should I do now?", he asked.

"Oh . . . um . . . we meet at the same time next week
and do the same thing again all over again," the vicar
suggested.

Why was the young man not helped to understand the
claims of Jesus and shown how he could enter a
relationship with God? I hope it was not because the
vicar thought that going to church and going through a
form of worship satisfy God.

The first thing to remember is that it is pointless to try

and establish your own level of goodness or religiosity so that you may be acceptable to God. We can never achieve the pass mark, which is perfection. Jesus told a parable to make this point very clear:

> To some who were confident of their own righteousness and looked down on everybody else, Jesus told this parable: "Two men went up to the temple to pray, one a Pharisee and the other a tax collector. The Pharisee stood up and prayed about himself: 'God, I thank you that I am not like other men – robbers, evildoers, adulterers – or even like this tax collector. I fast twice a week and give a tenth of all I get.'
>
> "But the tax collector stood at a distance. He would not even look up to heaven, but beat upon his breast and said, 'God have mercy on me, a sinner.'
>
> "I tell you that this man, rather than the other, went home justified before God. For everyone who exalts himself will be humbled, and he who humbles himself will be exalted."
>
> *(Luke 18:9–14)*

This explains why there will only be "sinners" in heaven. Those who recognise how self-centred they are may throw themselves on God and beg his mercy. Those who think they are reasonably all right and better than many will not lower themselves!

There was a lady who was a regular churchgoer, who approached her vicar for some help. She realised that she did not enjoy a relationship with God as she had seen in others and wondered why this was. After talking the problem over, the vicar summarised what he thought the problem was: "We have different religions! Yours is a DO religion; you try to impress God and others by your behaviour. Mine is a DONE religion. I have realised that I am in desperate need of a Saviour if I am to have hope of a relationship with God. I turned to Jesus and he has given me the forgiveness I need."

The prime response God asks of us is that we should turn our backs on our old lives and approach Jesus, asking him for forgiveness. When we do this, he will give us the gift of his Spirit that is the guarantee that we have been accepted by God.

How to respond – commit yourself to Jesus

If you have not definitely taken this step of faith and would like to, or if you would like to renew your commitment, will you please take a few moments to pray this matter through with him. Here is the type of prayer that all Christians have echoed in their hearts:

> Lord Jesus Christ,
> I have been living for myself and, till now, have left you, my rightful Lord, out of my life;
> I do need your forgiveness. I am willing to turn away from what is wrong in my life and start a new life with you,
> Thank you that you came to this earth and died to take away my sins. Come into my life and be my Lord for ever.

> Change me into the sort of person You
> want me to be.

That is the beginning! Jesus Christ has promised: "To all who received him, to those who believed in his name, he gave the right to become children of God" (John 1:12).

If you have turned to God and really mean to live a new life with and in obedience to the Lord Jesus, then you are forgiven and the effects of the Holy Spirit in your life will begin to appear in your life. Your new life has begun.

> Therefore, if anyone is in Christ, he is a new
> creation; the old has gone, the new has come!
> All this is from God, who reconciled us to
> himself through Christ.
> *(2 Corinthians 5:17–18)*

What if there is no obvious difference after opening your life to Jesus? Many years ago, a short man called Mr Falconer was working as a missionary to the sailors at Port Chalmers in New Zealand. He had just finished a short service for the seamen, which was held in a large loft used to store the ship's sails. A young sailor, Frank Bullen, stayed behind to talk. Frank explained that he did believe and had prayed a prayer of commitment to Jesus as his Saviour and Lord, but no obvious change had occurred, and he felt no assurance that he had been accepted by God. Mr Falconer read him one of the important sayings of Jesus: " I tell you the truth, whoever hears my word and believes him who sent me has eternal life and will not be condemned; he has crossed over from death to life" (John 5:24).

"Ah, I see how it is," exclaimed Mr Falconer, "you are waiting for the witness of your feelings to the truth of him who is himself the Truth. You dare not take him at his word unless your feelings, which are subject to a thousand changes a day, corroborate it. You must believe him *in spite* of your feelings and act accordingly."

Frank Bullen recorded many years later, "In a moment the hidden mystery was made clear to me, and I said quietly, 'I see, sir; it is the credibility of God against the witness of my feelings. Then I believe God!'"

"Let us thank God," answered the little missionary and they knelt down and prayed. Little more was said. There was no extravagant joy, or effervescent enthusiasm, but just a quiet satisfaction of having "found one's way after a long groping in darkness and misery".

The real proof that the Holy Spirit is active is the presence of a new priority – a desire to live for and with Jesus!

*"What difference does living
as a Christian make?
Would others notice?"*

Chapter 9

WHERE DO I
GO FROM HERE?

What happens now?

This chapter will only be relevant to a person who has repented, has asked Jesus to be his Lord and Saviour and is intent on developing this new relationship. This change in direction may be associated with great relief and excitement, but sometimes such feelings are absent.

However, those who have opened their lives to Jesus Christ will have noticed the following effects of God's Spirit in their life, or they will very soon!

Here are some changes that Christians have passed on.

Reading God's word
"I longed to understand my Bible. Reading it was no longer a chore. The words had a new living vibrancy."

Wanting to meet other Christians
"When I became a Christian I needed to meet up with other Christians. I joined a fellowship group attached to the church and went to every meeting I possibly could."

Prayer life
"Prayer took on a whole new meaning. It has become exciting to involve God personally in all that I do through prayer. I have an expectancy that God will work in a situation when I ask him."

Getting involved
"Although I knew I had a lot to learn I was keen to get involved with the business of living for God. My ears strained for something to do. Visiting an elderly man in the village became a real privilege. I knew I was in the right place and because I wanted to give, God taught me so much and I received so much from this small act."

This is God at work. All true Christians will experience something of those new desires.

After Peter's first sermon in Jerusalem, three thousand people became Christians. They were baptised publicly in the name of Jesus; they were not secretive about their new allegiance. In the same way, new Christians today need to align themselves with him openly. Do tell someone as soon as you can what has happened. These early Christians then: " . . . devoted themselves to the apostles' teaching and to the fellowship, to the breaking of bread and to prayer" (Acts 2:42).

Notice that this is the same as the comments above. Let us examine these four activities that the early Christians devoted themselves to.

1. The apostles' teaching

It is significant that this is mentioned first. The apostles claimed that they were teaching just what Jesus had taught them, and were therefore passing on the words of God. Thus, Peter wrote: "I want you to recall the words spoken in the past by the holy prophets and the command given by our Lord and Saviour through your apostles" (2 Peter 3:2).

The apostles were clear that their teaching had the same authority, God's authority, as the Old Testament writings. Devotion to the apostles' teaching is therefore the same as a devotion to Jesus' teaching. We have the apostles' teaching recorded in the Bible. For any book to be included in the New Testament, the early Christians had to be certain that it was apostolic in origin. For example, of the four gospels, two – Matthew and John – were written by the apostles themselves. Mark's gospel was a record of Peter's teaching made by his assistant, and Luke's gospel is Paul's teaching.

As in those early days, this is a striking feature that characterises a true Christian. They will want to know more of the Bible. Bishop J. C. Ryle, in his excellent book, *Practical Religion*, wrote:

There never was a man or woman truly converted, from one end of the world to the other, who did not love the revealed will of God. Just as a child born into the world desires naturally the milk provided for its nourishment, so does a soul "born again" desire the sincere milk of the Word. This is a common mark of all the children of God – they "delight in the law of the Lord" (Psalm 1:2).

Show me a person who despises Bible reading, or thinks little of Bible preaching, and I hold it to be a certain fact that he is not yet "born again". He may be zealous about forms and ceremonies. He may be diligent in attending sacraments and daily services. But, if these things are more precious to him than the Bible, I cannot think he is a converted man. Tell me what the Bible is to a man, and I will generally tell you what he is. This is the pulse to try – this is the barometer to look at – if we would know the state of the heart. I have no notion of the Spirit dwelling in a man and not giving clear evidence of his presence. And I believe it to be a signal evidence of the Spirit's presence when the Word is really precious to a man's soul.

Why is the Bible so important? It is because it is the inspired "Word of God": God-breathed. Jesus confirms that every word of scripture is given by God. It is perfect in its accuracy and sure in its dependability. Throughout the Old Testament times, God's people were always commanded to live according to the teaching of God. When the Jewish people left their captivity in Egypt under Moses, they were reminded that this was their priority. God gave them some special food called *Manna*, not just to stop them being hungry, but to teach his people this essential lesson:

> He humbled you, causing you to hunger and then feeding you with manna, which neither you nor your fathers had known, to teach you that man does not live on bread alone but on every word that comes from the mouth of the Lord.
>
> *(Deuteronomy 8:3)*

This passage was quoted by Jesus when he was tempted in the wilderness soon after his baptism; he regarded the Old Testament as being from God.

The longest chapter in the Bible, Psalm 119, is all about this theme. Of its 176 verses, all but four mention God's word, commands, laws, precepts, promises, statutes, decrees or the like. It is well worth reading, as it emphasises so clearly the priority God's word should have in our lives. Thus:

> I delight in your decrees;
>   I will not neglect your word.
>   *(Psalm 119:16)*

> Trouble and distress have come upon me,
>   but your commands are my delight.
> Your statutes are for ever right;

give me understanding that I may live.
(Psalm 119:143–4)

The prophet Daniel had been exiled into Babylon, and yet even there he regularly read the Scriptures which were the guide to the way he lived. In about 535 BC, he read something very relevant from the book of Jeremiah: "I, Daniel, understood from the Scriptures, according to the word of the Lord given to Jeremiah the prophet, that the desolation of Jerusalem would last seventy years. So I turned to the Lord God and pleaded with him in prayer . . . " (Daniel 9:2–3).

There can be no doubt that right from the beginning of time God intended his people to be followers of his word.

Jesus himself knew the Old Testament very well indeed, and is constantly quoting it as the absolute authority when discussing what God has done and requires of us. He frequently used the phrases, "Have you not read?" or "Have you not heard?" or "It is written," with regard to the Old Testament. He said to his disciples:

> Do not think that I have come to abolish the Law or the Prophets; I have not come to abolish them but to fulfil them. I tell you the truth, until heaven and earth disappear, not the smallest letter, not the least stroke of a pen, will by any means disappear from the Law until everything is accomplished.
> *(Matthew 5:17–18)*

Jesus never hesitated to rebuke those who thought other teachings to be of equal or higher value than the scriptures.

On one occasion he said to some religious leaders: "Why do you break the command of God for the sake of your tradition? ... Thus you nullify the word of God for the sake of your tradition" (Matthew 15:3, 6).

The same attitude to the scriptures is seen in the other New Testament writings. When Paul wrote to young Timothy, to whom he was passing on his responsibilities for the early churches, he says:

> But as for you, continue in what you have learned and have become convinced of, because you know those from whom you learned it, and how from infancy you have known the holy Scriptures, which are able to make you wise for salvation through faith in Christ Jesus. All Scripture is God-breathed and is useful for teaching, rebuking, correcting and training in righteousness, so that the man of God may be thoroughly equipped for every good work.
>
> *(2 Timothy 3:14–16)*

Peter was of the same mind, writing: "Above all, you must understand that no prophecy of Scripture came about by the prophet's own interpretation. For prophecy never had its origin in the will of man, but men spoke from God as they were carried along by the Holy Spirit" (2 Peter 1:20).

Peter again makes it clear that apostolic writing had the same authority as the old Jewish scriptures, when he writes about Paul's letters: " . . . our dear brother Paul also wrote to you with the wisdom that God gave him . . . his letters contain some things that are hard to understand, which ignorant and unstable people distort, as they do the other Scriptures, to their own destruction" (2 Peter 3:15–16).

When God's plan with regard to Jesus had been fully revealed, twenty-nine more books were added to the Old Testament to complete God's revelation. God's completed word was still authoritative, and to reject this authority will have eternal awful consequences.

All these godly men had a very high regard for scripture, clearly seeing it as the "Word of God". If people do not want to live according to his teaching, they are not God's people, they are not Christians, even though they may even be church officials! There are many religious people around but the great need is for people who think in God's way, who have "the mind of Christ". This will only happen by reading and studying the Bible. God's Spirit will then help us apply what we learn so that we do begin to think in God's way.

How can we learn God's word?
(a) Corporately After Pentecost, the first three thousand Christians learnt God's word by being taught it. Their teachers were the apostles who themselves had been taught by Jesus. This system has not changed. It is vital that every person who turns to Christ finds someone to teach them the Bible. This is the prime responsibility of the preachers in the churches. Their job is to explain and teach the scriptures, not to put forward their own ideas!

When I was in Hungary recently, I went to hear one of the national church leaders, his sermon being translated by a student who sat next to me. All was going well, until she suddenly stopped translating. I turned to her with a puzzled look on my face. She then said, "He has stopped teaching us the Bible now and is giving his own opinions instead." That student knew what preaching should be. She understood something of what God meant when, speaking through an Old Testament prophet, he strongly reproached the preachers of that era: "The lips of a priest ought to preserve knowledge, and from his mouth men ought to seek instruction – because he is the messenger of the Lord Almighty. But you have turned from the way and by your teaching have caused many to stumble" (Malachi 2:7–8).

When looking for a teacher, therefore, do make sure it is someone who reveres and teaches the whole authentic word of God revealed in the Bible. What the Bible says, God says. Shun a church or person who does not see this as his priority.

The smaller home Bible study group can be especially helpful and all new Christians are strongly encouraged to get involved with one of these, if at all possible. The teaching can be much more personal and specific questions can be answered in a way that is seldom possible in a sermon! Similarly, one-to-one tutoring will help a new Christian understand and learn new ideas and practices even more quickly.

(b) Individually It has always been a scriptural principle that Christians need to spend some time every day reading and thinking about part of the Bible. This applies to all, from the greatest to the smallest. Kings are not excused! God gave special instructions to the future kings of his people on this subject:

> When he takes the throne of his kingdom,
> he is to write for himself on a scroll of paper
> a copy of this law, taken from that of the

priests, who are Levites. It is to be with him,
and he is to read it all the days of his life so
that he may learn to revere the Lord his God
and follow carefully all the words of this law
and these decrees, and not consider himself
better than his brothers and turn from the
law to the right or to the left.

(Deuteronomy 17:18–20)

Many years later, a psalmist wrote: "Oh, how I love
your law! I meditate on it all day long" (Psalm 119:97).

So, today, for the same reasons, each Christian should
be encouraged to make Bible study a high personal
priority. There are several different daily study notes or
books available to help do this systematically, and advice
on this will be available from someone in your church or
from a Bible bookshop.

After the death of Robert Louis Stevenson (author of
Treasure Island), his Bible was found. Someone noted
that Psalm 34:5 had been rubbed away – the reason was
that the verse above, verse 4, was his favourite. His finger
had traced the familiar words so often that the print below
had all but vanished!

I sought the Lord, and he answered me;
    he delivered me from all my fears.

It is a wise new Christian who learns to rely on his
daily Bible study to bring him closer to the Master that
he longs to know and serve. Similarly it is a wise parent
who reads portions of the Bible every day with their
children and talks over its implications.

2. The fellowship

This word has been cheapened by Western churches to become little more than a friendship circle. The original Greek word *koinonia* meant much more. It was derived from the Greek word *koinos* meaning "common". Firstly, it was a business term signifying partnership. Two or more people would work together for a common business purpose. It can also be used to describe a selfless approach to communal life. For these reasons, it was often applied to a marriage where a couple joined with common purpose in a selfless way.

It is not surprising therefore that this word was used to describe the association of Christians. They joined together in groups to encourage and help each other selflessly to live for Jesus and to make the gospel known. All new Christians join the people of God with this purpose. There cannot be solitary Christians, living for God their own way, and on their own.

This biblical view of church membership means that all Christians should be actively involved in one or more aspects of their local church. There is no room for passengers.

The early church in Jerusalem recognised this need for being active Christians as they were " . . . enjoying the favour of all the people. And the Lord added to their number daily those who were being saved" (Acts 2:47).

There are always needs in the local church, such as helping in the home groups or Sunday school, visiting those with problems or helping with administration or catering. We may also be able to share material goods or skills we have been given. Remember, however, that the main business of the church is to encourage its members to live godly lives and to make his gospel known.

Kate Booth, wife of General Booth, the founder of the Salvation Army, was addressing a comfortable group of church-goers when she said indignantly, "Is that all you do for a dying world – you go to church!"

It can be daunting trying to learn new skills, such as how to share the message of Jesus with others. Some seem to be waiting on the sidelines, looking on but not getting involved. No one learns this way; we need to step out and try. There was once some very bad advice given to a youngster: "Don't get into the water until you have learnt to swim."

3. The breaking of bread

This was obviously very important to the early Christians as it was again mentioned in verse 46, where the practice is explained: "They broke bread in their homes and ate together with glad and sincere hearts, praising God " (Acts 2:46–47).

What a wonderful glimpse of what fellowship meant. It has been said to young Christians when looking for a good church to join, "Look out for a church where God's word is taught, and where they invite you back for a meal"!

However our original verse (v. 42) suggests that there was more going on at these meals than just befriending. They praised God, remembering what Jesus had done by dying for them on the Cross. These were the beginning of our Communion service or "Lord's Supper", but were much more informal and were full of natural praise. What a need there is today for Christians to use their homes to invite people in for coffee or a meal, where they can see our joy at being accepted by God. We are called upon to open our homes, not just to friends but even strangers, and make them feel at home.

4. Prayer

All Christians need to develop a habit of prayer. This should also, like Bible study, be both corporate and individual.

a) Praying Together

The early Christians continued to meet every day in the temple courts. Doubtless the temple services must have seemed rather austere and formal, and they did not mention Jesus – but the Christians continued to meet there and praise God corporately. Doubtless they did also use the occasion to share the gospel with others; they certainly engaged in some open-air preaching!

There is a lesson for us here, in that although very few church services are ideal, it is vital for all Christians to **continue** to meet up corporately, so that the body of Christians in an area thank God together for what he has done. When they stop meeting up in this way, it can often be a sign that they are slipping away from their allegiance to Christ. Small informal groups are extremely helpful, but should not replace the larger gathering of all God's people. There they can praise God together, encourage the other Christians, be a witness to that society, and hear the Bible well taught.

> And let us consider how we may spur one
> another on towards love and good deeds. Let
> us not give up meeting together, as some are

in the habit of doing, but let us encourage
one another – and all the more as you see
the Day approaching.

(Hebrews 10:24–5)

b) Personal Prayer

Praying throughout the day is undoubtedly the key to
staying close to the Lord. It is not always necessary to
shut our eyes! We can learn what God has done for us
and what he expects of us from the Bible, but we keep
the relationship warm by prayer. Whenever there are
problems, tell your Lord; when you have failed him,
apologise quickly, and when something goes well, thank
him. There is also great value in specifying a particular
time every day for personal prayer. It is otherwise all too
easy for personal prayer to be eased out of a busy life. It
has been well said that "Seven prayerless days makes one
weak." If you want a good test of your commitment to
Jesus, measure your prayer life. What a person is alone
before God is really all that he is! Many Christians
combine their time of Bible reading and prayer, calling it
a "Quiet Time".

The apostle Paul frequently stresses this priority. He
used to pray daily for those Christians he was concerned
for, and encouraged others to do the same: "Devote
yourselves to prayer, being watchful and thankful"
(Colossians 4:2).

Talking problems over with God and seeking his
intervention can have powerful results. John Knox was a
preacher who was deeply involved in bringing about a
spiritual awakening in Scotland, but it was his prayer life
that was the key. It was said that his prayers were "the
greatest event in Scottish history".

It is not the volume of prayer that makes prayer effective – it is the person whom we are speaking to that matters. Jesus, the sustainer and creator of the universe, is able and willing to act for his glory. Just as the value of faith depends completely on whether the object of that faith is real and effective, so prayer is a waste of time if Jesus is not involved.

Chapter 10

YOU CAN MAKE
A DIFFERENCE!

Recently I was introduced to a lady in her late thirties who was visiting one of my patients in hospital.

"She has recently been confirmed," my patient informed me.

"That's great," I replied, and turning to her friend said, "but may I ask you 'Are you sure you are now a Christian?' "

She thought for a moment and replied hesitatingly, "Well, I am trying to live as one."

As the conversation continued it became obvious that she was not clear of the distinction between:

1.   how a person becomes a Christian;

2.   what a person then does to live the Christian life.

She was hoping that because she lived a reasonably good life and had joined a church, that somehow this might be enough to please God. She had not grasped that all of us are helpless sinful people and that there is nothing that we can offer God to make peace with him. What a joy it was to explain that our relationship with God depends solely on what Jesus has done on the Cross, and that our responsibility starts after we have appreciated that we have been graciously given this new life as a free gift. She was not sure of her relationship with God because she felt that somehow it depended on what she did!

Martin Luther was a very bright young lawyer in the sixteenth century who became an Augustinian monk at the age of twenty-one. He became increasingly aware that however hard he tried, he was still very much a sinner, and that even the most obsessional confession of even the most minor misdemeanours did not bring him peace. At one stage his confessor became fed up and said, "Look here, if you expect Christ to forgive you, come with something to forgive – patricide, blasphemy, adultery – instead of all these peccadilloes." Luther became more and more distraught. "My situation was that although an impeccable monk, I stood before God as a sinner troubled in conscience and I had no confidence that my merit would assuage him."

Martin Luther was then appointed as Professor of Bible at the small local University of Wittenberg, and he set himself to learn the Scriptures so that he could teach them well. His eyes were then gradually opened to understand the gospel. When studying the Psalms for his first series of lectures, he was struck by Psalm 22, with its opening words, "My God, my God, why have you forsaken me?" Why was it that the perfect Jesus felt this same separation from God that he himself constantly felt? The light began to dawn – Christ had taken his own sin. Jesus had been separated from his father in heaven because he had borne Martin Luther's sin! What a revelation this was! God was not an angry austere inhuman God, but one who had such an overflowing love for us that through Jesus he himself had made it possible for anyone to be at one with God himself. Luther became a Christian when he understood and accepted what Jesus had done for him. Then he knew he was free of sin. The realisation that God loves me as I am and has forgiven me is the root from which the Christian life grows.

Martin Luther clearly understood this difference between becoming a Christian and living as a Christian when he said: "Faith is the root, works are the shoot."

There are some who try to behave in a Christian way, without having established a root of reliance on Jesus. They will not be satisfied, and eventually the shoot will dry up and die. Conversely, however, if there is no shoot of a Christian life appearing, then almost certainly there is no true root.

This distinction between becoming a Christian and living the Christian life is frequently found in the Bible.

> For it is by grace you have been saved, through faith – and this is not from your-selves, it is the gift of God – not by works,

> so that no one can boast. For we are Christ's
> workmanship, created in Christ Jesus to do
> good works, which God prepared in advance
> for us to do.
>
> *(Ephesians 2:8–10)*

Note the tenses here: we **have been** saved simply by trusting Jesus, but from then on there **are** good works that God wants us to do.

Exactly the same distinction is taught at the end of the letter to Titus, whom Paul had left in Crete to establish the new churches there.

> But when the kindness and love of God our
> Saviour appeared, he saved us, not because
> of righteous things we had done, but because
> of his mercy. He saved us through the
> washing of rebirth and renewal by the Holy
> Spirit, whom he poured out on us generously
> through Jesus Christ our Saviour, so that
> having been justified by his grace, we might
> become heirs having the hope of eternal life.
> This is a trustworthy saying. And I want
> you to stress these things, so that those who
> have trusted in God may be careful to devote
> themselves to doing what is good.
>
> *(Titus 3:4–8)*

Note that when we start the new life, or are reborn, we receive the Holy Spirit who inspires the new lifestyle. The Holy Spirit is not just a theological doctrine; he is a life-changing power. If no change is occurring, then it is doubtful whether this power is present.

Never forget, however, that Christian good works, which are essential in Christian people, can never bring us into a right relationship with God. I have stressed this point deliberately as it has probably always been one of the most misunderstood aspects of Bible teaching.

What are the features of a Christian life?

Just as the shoots of most new seedlings have two leaflets, so there are two main areas that Christians need to develop, and these are repeatedly stressed in the Bible. They are:

1.   to be holy;

2.   to share Jesus.

Peter's first letter was written when he was imprisoned in Rome with the prospect of execution looming ahead for him. At this time many of the young churches were shifting away from Christ's teaching and these letters are his attempt to make matters clear as to what God wants. Amazingly there is no hint of depression, in spite of his difficult situation.

Peter begins with a remarkable paragraph – full of praise to God, because of the permanent new life that Jesus has secured for his people:

> Praise be to the God and Father of our Lord Jesus Christ! In his great mercy he has given us new birth into a living hope through the resurrection of Jesus Christ from the dead,

and into an inheritance that can never perish
spoil or fade – kept in heaven for you.

(1 Peter 1:3–4)

What a terrific description of the confidence God wants us to have! All Christians should have this sense of assurance, knowing that they are forgiven, not because of their doings, but because of what their Saviour has done for them. Here the root is emphasised.

Following this introduction Peter goes on to urge his readers to build a new life, the shoot, on this foundation .

1. Be holy

Today some people think of "holiness" as an old-fashioned, unattractive, "holier than thou" religious attitude, but Peter pleads that we should all become holy because God is: "Be holy, because I am holy" (1 Peter 1:16).

It is clear that Peter understands holiness as being like Jesus! Jesus has given us as a gift the **status** of good, honest, God-centred people, and now he wants us to begin to make this a practical reality, by a determination to live his way: "As **obedient** children, do not conform to the evil desires you had when you lived in ignorance" (1 Peter 1:14).

This is the secret – to live in **obedience** to what God has taught us in the Bible. Just as it was by understanding the Bible's message that you became a Christian, so it is by obeying his word that we grow as Christians. We begin to think like Jesus. Some Christians seem to appear as just very negative people: they don't do this and they don't do that. This is a total misunderstanding of the Christian life. Jesus came to give us joy, kindness and peace. It is right, however, to have an abhorrence of wrongdoing, but hopefully the main characteristic of Christians will be more positive. We should be known for being good people, who are not spineless but behave like Jesus.

Do not sin   It is all too easy to put on a pretence of spirituality that may fool some. There was a *Crimewatch* programme on television in which the police were seeking help in solving a particularly nasty murder. The murdered man had been very involved with his local church, being its sacristan (the person who looks after the sacred vessels). The film first showed his religious duties in the church. They then revealed another side of his life. He was an active homosexual, heavily involved in local gay clubs, and known to be promiscuous. How horrible this double life appeared, so what must God think about it! He has stated again and again in the Bible that he finds such activities abhorrent.

> Do not be deceived: Neither the sexually immoral nor idolaters nor adulterers nor male prostitutes nor homosexual offenders nor thieves nor the greedy nor drunkards nor slanderers nor swindlers will inherit the kingdom of God.
>
> *(1 Corinthians 6:9–10)*

These are not the features of those who have God's Spirit in them. We are told instead, "Be holy in all you do" (1 Peter 1:15). It is all too easy to try and keep certain areas out of God's control.

Sarah was a teenager involved with her local church youth group. She had a boyfriend who was not a Christian and, as happens so often today, they were in the habit of sleeping together. She went on a church weekend youth conference and was enjoying it very much until there was a talk on boyfriend/girlfriend relationships. The speaker showed some of the biblical passages that showed clearly that sex outside marriage was considered wrong by God. He also emphasised the Bible teaching that Christians should only marry Christians. This upset Sarah, so she went up to the speaker afterwards and tried to explain that today things are different!

The speaker went over the biblical teaching again. It became clear that Sarah liked the theory of Jesus being her Saviour, but did not want him to be anything more than that. In fact she disagreed with Jesus' teaching in the area of sex. The wise speaker explained to her that it was not possible to have Jesus as Saviour without him being Lord as well. He took a piece of paper and wrote on it two words:

NO LORD

He explained that if we say NO to God, then he is no longer our Lord and Saviour. If we say Jesus is our LORD, then we will do what he says. Sarah was given a pen and he gently suggested that she go to her room, think this matter through, and decide which of the two words she wanted to delete. It was a very difficult half hour for Sarah, but she then returned, smiling, to the speaker. She had crossed off the word NO!

For many of us the main problem may not be sexual; it may be how we talk about other people – there is a great emphasis on this in the New Testament, warning us to be very careful with our tongues. The problem may be whether we are willing to be known publicly as Christians, or it may even be how we regard some doctrines in the Bible. To accept Jesus however, means to accept his teaching. Jesus himself said:

> If anyone is ashamed of me and of my words, the Son of Man will be ashamed of him when he comes in glory.
>
> *(Luke 9:26)*

> Whoever has my commands and obeys them – he is the one who loves me.
>
> *(John 14:21)*

Yes, we are called to be holy and not to sin. It is important to remember that sin is not just doing wrong things. Sin can also be a failure to do what is good or kind. Christians should be good people.

Be good In the second half of Peter's first epistle, he gives practical advice as to how Christ's followers should behave in different circumstances. There is a section about relationships with all human authorities, and the Christians are reminded: "For it is God's will that by doing good you should silence the ignorant talk of foolish men" (1 Peter 2:15).

In the next section advising slaves, Peter says: "But if you suffer for doing good and you endure it, this is commendable before God" (1 Peter 2:20).

This theme continues throughout chapters 2 and 3, where the word "good" is used nine times to describe the lives of Christians. Our lives should be attractive.

A Japanese Christian once wrote, "I read in a book that Jesus went about doing good. What concerns me is that I am so easily satisfied just going about."

Keep it up   There will often be temptations to return
to old ways – "just this once!" Do not listen. One of our
problems is that we do like to dabble with sin. We enjoy
chewing ideas over in our minds that we know do not
please Jesus. Part of us wants to throw them out of our
lives, but another part of us wants to call out as they leave,
"What's your telephone number?"

The devil will also try and fill you with guilt for past
wrongdoings. All those things are forgiven and forgotten
by God, so don't allow them to be raked up again.

There was an old West Indian preacher who was
emphasising this point. He cried out to his congregation,
quoting Micah 7:19: "God has thrown all your sins into
the deepest sea, and he has put up a notice: N O
F I S H I N G"!

We will frequently fail, but as in any loving relationship
the secret is to say sorry and start again as if nothing went
wrong. Too often Christians slip up and find themselves
sitting in a puddle, feeling bad about what has happened.
The secret is to get up and start again; the mistake is to sit
there wallowing in self-pity and failure.

2. Share Jesus

Right from the earliest days all Christians were expected
to be involved in helping others see that Jesus is the truth,
and that everyone needs him. The great commission to
the disciples was:

> Go ye therefore, and teach all nations,
> baptising them in the name of the Father,
> and of the Son, and of the Holy Ghost:
> Teaching them to observe all things surely

whatsoever I have commanded you: and, lo,
I am with you always, even unto the end of
the world.

(Matthew 28:19–20 AV)

Some have suggested that this command to share the
gospel with all people was primarily directed at the
disciples, but if you read the text again it is apparent that
the new Christians are expected to continue living just as
the first disciples did. It is as we embark on the task of
sharing the gospel with others that we will know God's
power is with us. One preacher put it clearly saying, "No
go, no lo!"

Peter made it abundantly clear that all ordinary
Christians should be involved in sharing the gospel with
others.

But you are a chosen people, a royal
priesthood, a holy nation, a people belonging
to God, that you may declare the praises of
him who called you out of darkness into his
wonderful light.

(1 Peter 2:9)

We are now God's special people, as the Jewish people
were in Old Testament times. This verse also teaches
that we are each members of the Royal family. In pre-
Christian times God instituted a system of priests who
acted as intermediaries between himself and the people.
It was not possible to worship God without having a priest.
You would take your sacrifice to the holy place where
the priest, a holy man, would make the sacrifice on your
behalf. In this passage Peter makes it clear that all

Christians now have this role. We are the intermediaries who are to act as signposts, directing people so that they can find peace with God. This is both a great privilege and a great responsibility.

There is a church in Wimbledon that attracts many students. Each term it has a card describing the church activities and on the back the church officers are listed. One of these began, "Ministers – the whole congregation," and then names the vicar and curates and others. They recognise that it is the ordinary Christians who are to be the key communicators and ministers of the church. This is not to say that we don't need good church leaders who will teach, train and encourage their church members to fulfil their responsibilities in building up God's church. This particularly applies to the areas of helping others become Christians and then helping them mature as Christians.

The life of a church is directly related to its concern to share the message about Jesus and the salvation he offers. A Christian does not choose to be in the business of bringing people to Christ; he chooses Christ and is at once in the business!

How can we share Jesus with others?

It is vital that all new Christians openly acknowledge their new allegiance. Conversations about Jesus will then follow. If you are asked, "Do anything interesting last night?" when you were out at a Bible study group, you can either reply with a vague "No," or more positively, "Yes, I have just started going to a group that are studying what Jesus and his disciples taught." Nothing will help people to think more than that! The subsequent questions may be difficult to answer but will be a great incentive to do some studying. This idea of doing some Christian "prep" or homework is not new either. In the same epistle Peter urges his readers to do some homework so that they can help any people who inquire about the Christian way and explain why they have started on it.

> But in your hearts set apart Christ as Lord.
> Always be *prepared* to give an answer to
> everyone who asks you to give the reason
> for the hope that you have. But do this with
> gentleness and respect.
> *(1 Peter 3:15, emphasis added)*

How wise that last sentence is. There is no point in giving even the most brilliant answer if it is given in such a way as to turn the listener away from what you are saying. We must not talk as arrogant "know-alls", but share the good news just as "one beggar telling another beggar where to find food"! Tact is the ability to get your point across without stabbing someone with it!

The other way to help people to consider the Christian claims is to invite them to some event where the claims of Christ are to be discussed. Peter himself became interested in Jesus when his brother Andrew became a disciple of Jesus. The first thing that Andrew did was to find Peter and say, "We have found the Messiah," and he brought Peter to Jesus. I was introduced to Christian things at university when I was invited by some Christian friends to join them at some special sermons in a church, geared to help students think through these issues. How grateful I am to those friends. Another idea is to have small "supper parties" and invite some friends round to look at the Christian claims and hear what has happened to you. It might be possible to have an older Christian with you to help out with any sticky questions!

Twice a year we have an "Open Supper" in our home and we invite neighbours, friends, colleagues at work and patients. We have an appetising buffet meal and then sit down to listen to an after-dinner speaker whose role is to help people to start thinking about Jesus. Discussions in informal groups, over coffee, inevitably follow. After the first two of these people came up to us afterwards and said something like, "That makes you think," but we saw very few people become Christians. We then introduced a Christian Basics course to follow each open supper. The syllabus of this five-week course is roughly what is in this book. The response was dramatic, and now many people have become Christians over the last twelve years because of these.

There are many similar ideas, but it is seldom the lack of ideas that prevent such things happening; it is usually a lack of will to see things happen!

Paul also emphasised these two main tasks of being holy and sharing Jesus with others. At the beginning of his letter to the Philippians he summarises his prayer: "So that you may be able to discern what is best and may be pure and blameless until the day of Christ, filled   with the fruit of righteousness that comes through Jesus Christ" (Philippians 1:10–11).

He is obviously concerned that the main feature of their lives should be holiness. In the next paragraph however he deals with the theme of letting others know the gospel, and how his imprisonment has, in a roundabout way, helped achieve this end:

Now I want you to know, brothers, that what has happened to me has really served to advance the gospel. As a result it has become clear throughout the whole palace guard and to everyone else that I am in chains for Christ. Because of my chains, most of the brothers in the Lord have been encouraged to speak the word of God more courageously and fearlessly.

(Philippians 1:12–14)

It is interesting to read that the early Christians had just the same problems as modern Christians and that they did not find it easy to talk about Jesus either.

Set your goal and go for it

In England four out of five churches are getting smaller and older (the church is the group of Christian people, not the building!). We are now living in a society that has little interest in God and is becoming increasingly selfish. Divorces are on the increase, and our prisons are overflowing. The law will not be able to stem the tide; the change of direction will only come when individual Christians begin to take the gospel seriously again. Society will benefit as a result.

During the first World War, Marshal Foch was commanding part of the allied army at the Battle of the Marne. The battle was not going well, but he telegraphed to headquarters: "The main body of our army is giving way – the left is in retreat, but I am attacking just the same."

We know that Christ will eventually win and that we

shall then stand with him in heaven, and this is the great incentive for us to forget past failures and determine to make pleasing Jesus our absolute priority. The apostle Paul saw it this way:

> But one thing I do: Forgetting what is behind and straining towards what is ahead, I press on toward the goal to win the prize for which God has called me heavenward in Christ Jesus.
>
> *(Philippians 3:13–14)*

There is a tombstone in the Alps of a climber killed in an accident. It simply says: "He died climbing."

What a great epitaph for a Christian!

Help is at hand

These standards of Christian behaviour may sound rather daunting, but it is important to remember that when we decide to turn off the broad way and start the new life with Jesus, we are each given a remarkable gift – the presence of the Spirit of God himself. He will motivate us to want to do God's will, and will empower us to achieve this. This is what Jesus has said on the subject:

> If you love me, you will obey what I command. And I will ask the Father, and he will give you another Counsellor to be with you for ever – the Spirit of truth. The world cannot accept him, because it neither sees him nor knows him. But you know him, for he lives with you and will be in you. I will

not leave you as orphans; I will come to you.
(John 14:15–18)

What a wonderful promise, but note that the Holy Spirit is only available to those who are committed to obeying what Jesus commands. Determine to stay close to Jesus, relying on what he has completed for us, doing what he wants, and you will experience the power of his Spirit in your life. As your relationship deepens with him you will experience a joy and a purpose that permeates every aspect of your lives. Gradually your character will become more like that of Jesus, and will demonstrate his love, his joy, his peace, his patience, his kindness – the fruit of his Spirit being present as outlined in 2 Peter 1:3–9.

Albert McMakin was a twenty-four-year-old American farmer. He had not been a Christian very long, but he already longed for his friends to discover the Saviour he had found. There was a mission taking place at a nearby town so he borrowed a lorry to take him and his friends. One of his good friends was not interested. He was tall and handsome and he had other loves! Albert prayed that God would act. In the end his friend was persuaded to drive the lorry for them! At the mission this friend joined the others and was enthralled by what he heard. He had never heard this before. It was so relevant to him. He returned night after night, until one evening he could resist the draw of God no longer and invited Jesus to be his Saviour and Lord. That young man was called Billy Graham. Since then Billy has helped many thousands of others to find a relationship with God through Jesus. That is the work of the Holy Spirit. He enthused Albert McMakin into wanting to win his friends, and helped him find a way so that they could hear the gospel. It is

God's Spirit that drew the disinterested Billy to himself, and who gave him the longing to use his life in his Saviour's service. God is not asleep. How we need to wake up to the fact that God is active, working both in response to the prayers of his family, and on his own initiative.

The Spirit of God always points people to Jesus. He has given us the Bible, which reveals "the mind of God" and makes its teaching relevant to us individually. It is he who enables Christians to serve Jesus, reminding us what pleases him, and empowering us to be bold for him.

Every Christian has been given at least one specific gift for building up God's people. One of our jobs is to find out what this is and develop it for the benefit of our church. The gifts vary widely from an ability to teach, an aptitude for administration, a passion for praying for others, special wisdom and insight, to being an encouragement and help to others. There is no end to the list, but they are always given for the benefit of the church.

We must not be gullible however. Some will claim to have spiritual gifts, but these may not be from God. We are told to test claims of the spirits. This we do by assessing the effects. A true work of God's Spirit will draw people to Jesus and the teaching of God.

> Dear friends, do not believe every spirit, but test the spirits to see whether they are from God, because many false prophets have gone out into the world. This is how you can recognise the Spirit of God: Every spirit that acknowledges Jesus Christ has come in the

flesh is from God, but every spirit that does
not acknowledge Jesus is not from God.

(1 John 4:1–3)

The strength that we need to stand firm in this difficult
world is given to us by the Holy Spirit.

You will receive power when the Holy
Spirit comes on you and you shall be my
witnesses . . .

(Acts 1:8)

Alexander Mackay, a Scottish engineer, went to
Uganda as the first missionary in 1877. He established a
workshop with an anvil, tools and a printing press, and
groups of young pages from the court of the Kabaka, the
King of Buganda, used to visit. There they would learn
about Jesus and many became committed Christians. In
1884 the king died and his son, Mwanga, was antagonistic
to the Christian faith. He was angry that the Christians
taught that there was a higher authority than the king,
particularly when this meant that the pages refrained from
the homosexual practices that were common in court life.
To demonstrate his authority he ordered the arrest of a
group of four pages who were on safari with Mackay.
The boys were captured by some soldiers, had their hands
bound with rope, and were marched back to the capital.
Despite pleas and gifts from Mackay, only his personal
servant was released; the other three were condemned to
be burned to death. There were many hundreds gathered
at their execution. The parents of the boys pleaded with
them to renounce their commitment to Jesus. They
refused, and instead started to sing hymns to their Saviour.

The youngest of these boys was Yusufu who said to his executioners, "Please don't cut off my arms, I will not struggle in the fire that takes me to Jesus." The effect of their execution was not what King Mwanga wanted. More people became Christians, and many more pages from the court were baptised.

Joseph Balikudembe was a senior page at court and was popular with Mwanga. He had become a Christian. When he heard of the King's decision to have the newly appointed Anglican bishop, James Hannington, murdered he complained to the king, reminding him that he would have to answer to God for such an action. Mwanga became very angry and Joseph was condemned to death by burning. Before he died he said to his executioner, "Tell Mwanga that I have been wrongly accused and unjustly condemned, but that he has my forgiveness. However, unless he repents of this deed, I shall be his accuser before the judgement seat of God."

The small church grew steadily in spite of this opposition. However, in 1886, Mwanga returned unexpectedly early from an unsuccessful hippopotamus hunt to find his pages in small groups studying the Bible. He was livid, claiming that the boys had been bewitched by the Christians. Other chiefs encouraged Mwanga to take a firm line, saying that they would find better servants if these were killed. The boys were all assembled and were told to divide into two groups, those who followed Christ and those who followed Mwanga. He was shocked to see so many join the Christian group and he hesitated from killing them all. Instead he randomly picked out several of them. The charge was "For following Christ." They were marched in pairs to the site of execution, twenty-two miles away from the capital. On June 3rd, 1886 these young Christian lads, Catholics and Anglicans, were tied in reed matting and the fires were lit. There was no screaming, just the crackle of the fires and a quiet sobbing. Then some singing and prayers broke the stillness. Only one man wailed; he was an executioner who had been forced to kill his own son, who was one of these Christian pages.

What had enabled these youngsters to stand so firmly against such opposition? It was the work of the same Holy Spirit who has helped Christians to stand up boldly for the truth and remain resolute however hard the going is. Jesus himself has promised.

Keep Jesus busy

It is unfortunately all too easy to get immersed in Christian activity and find that the relationship with Jesus quietly gets colder.

After I became a Christian, I became active in the Christian Unions at both my university and my medical school in London. I was a member of a thrilling church where the Bible teaching was exceptionally good. I was elected President of the Christian Union and we saw some remarkable things happen. A friend and I then went to Uganda to help with work in a mission hospital in Uganda. We were well taught and felt we had a lot to offer.

One afternoon my friend and I were strolling up Namirembe hill, in the centre of Kampala, when we met a Ugandan Christian coming down on the other side of the road. He had a broad smile with bright teeth, and a very deep dog collar round his neck. "Hello," he called.

We crossed over the road and started talking. "What

are you doing in Uganda?" he asked.

"We are working in Mengo Mission Hospital."

"Oh, that's lovely. Does that mean that you are Christians then?"

"Yes, we both are," we replied.

"That's good, but tell me, how are you getting on with Jesus?"

I had never been asked a question like that before, but gave a typical English reply, "Very well, thank you, and you?"

We may have blushed but somehow the Ugandan minister must have seen our embarrassment because he switched the conversation to himself, still with that open smile on his face, and said:

"I became a Christian when I was 29 years old and was working as a schoolmaster. I became very active in my church, but somehow, in spite of all my Christian activities, my walk with the Lord was cold. Then I learnt what the problem with me was. I was active for God but he was not closely involved in what I was doing. I then learnt to keep Jesus busy in all I was doing. If I failed him, I learnt to say sorry quickly; when everything was going well I learnt to keep thanking him; when there were problems I learnt to involve Jesus at the beginning. That's the secret I have learnt – to keep Jesus busy. I must go now, but please don't forget, keep Jesus busy." He then disappeared down the hill.

I have no idea who that Christian was, but one day in heaven I will thank him from the bottom of my heart for giving me those five minutes. That is the secret – it is not just obedience that God wants; above all, he longs for a close friendship with each of us.

A feeling of failure

It is important to remember that none of us will be perfect Christians. We will fail in countless numbers of ways, sometimes through deliberately doing things that are wrong, and at other times by just letting the relationship with Jesus slip. Just because we are Christians does not mean that our problems will go away. The unmarried mother will still have that child to look after. The patient with advanced cancer will still have to cope with his disease. The great difference is that we have a real friend in our heavenly Father who wants to share our problems and help us manage.

Sometimes when people first become Christians there is great excitement and peace. Everything seems wonderful – like a honeymoon. It is likely however that this elation will not persist in the same form, just as the love of a newly married couple will change and mature over the years. This is normal. Just because we are Christians it doesn't mean the end of stress, strain, exhaustion, fear, opposition, frustration, illness or anything else. There are two reasons for this. Firstly the devil now has a target and he will do all he can to dislodge the relationship we have with our Saviour and friend. Secondly, God wants us to mature and it is only through facing and overcoming problems that this will happen. Sometimes people will feel depressed and ineffective for God. The lesson to learn is to hang in there. Involve God in the problems and keep asking what he wants you to do.

If you are on a walk and you trip up and fall into a muddy puddle, the last thing to do is to just sit there moaning about your predicament. It is important to get up and carry on as you were before. Sometimes disasters can be used by God as his megaphone to tell us that we are drifting away from our walk with him. Such problems are common to us all. This is why it is vital that all Christians recognise that we are followers of Jesus, not because of what we receive, but primarily because it is true. When a person is convinced of the truth, he can have such a determination that whatever happens to him, he will continue to live with and in obedience to their Lord and Saviour.

Press on

Christians will have to face similar pressures to everyone else but they do know the direction they are going.

> One ship goes east, one ship goes west,
> By the self-same wind that blow,
> It's the set of the sails and not the gales
> That determines which way they go!

Our eternal destiny is not a matter of chance, it is a matter of choice.

David Livingstone was a doctor who spent his life as a missionary in central Africa. He died in 1873, in a native hut, his body wasted by colitis. He only met one white man in the last seven years of his life. That man was an American journalist, H. M. Stanley, who had come to find this remarkable Englishman. Stanley deeply admired Livingstone's Anglo-Saxon resolution never to relinquish his work, but he soon recognised that his strength was the deep commitment to Jesus as his Lord and Saviour. This is what Stanley wrote:

> His religion was not of the theoretical kind, but is a constant earnest sincere practice. In him religion exhibits its loveliest features; it governs his conduct not only towards his servants but towards the natives, the bigoted Mohammedans, and all who come in contact with him. Without it Livingstone with his ardent temperament, his enthusiasm, his high spirit and courage must have become uncompanionable, and a hard master. Religion had tamed him, and made him a Christian gentleman.

It is not surprising that Stanley was won for Christ by Livingstone.

You may not be called to be famous like Dr Livingstone, but we are all called to be resolute in our determination to live close to God, for his honour and not our own; to be good people, and share the message of God's salvation as widely as we can.

In the centre of Bristol is a statue of John Wesley, who did so much to draw the churches back to Christ's priorities. On the plinth are the simple words he frequently used, that motivated his life and should be the basis of every Christian's life:

"May I commend my Saviour to you?"

Cure for Life

Study Guide

The **Cure for Life** *Study Guide* is designed to accompany this book. In six one-hour-long sessions it covers all ten chapters, using a question and answer format to simulate discussion.

The sessions are run by one or two group leaders depending on the size of the group. Ideally there should be three to eight group members who are either new Christians or interested enquirers. Each week they read one or two chapters of **Cure for Life** to prepare them for the session.

The questions in the study guide are designed to get the group members to grapple with the material presented, to think through their individual response to it and to give them an opportunity to air their objections and questions about the Christian message.

The *Study Guide* comes in two formats. One for group members - containing questions - and one for group leaders - with extra discussion material.

Group Members – 12pp (A4 loose leaf format in plastic folder)
Single copy £2.00
5–10 copies (10% discount) £1.80
11–20 copies (25% discount) £1.50
21+ copies (35% discount) £1.30

Group Leaders – 37pp (A4 loose leaf format in plastic folder)
Single copy £3.00
All prices include postage & packing.

Available direct from:
Publications Dept, Christian Medical Fellowship
157 Waterloo Road, London SE1 8XN
Tel 020 7928 4694 Fax 020 7620 2453 Email pubs@cmf.org.uk